CAMINO
EASY

A stress-free planning guide for your first trek on the Camino de Santiago.

For mature walkers, with focus on a 1 or 2 week adventure.

Barry Sanders writing as:

B G Preston

Revised and updated October 2019

Important note regarding the Camino service offerings cited in this work. Simply put, they do change. As a result, it is advisable to check with any of the Camino companies to verify their exact and current offerings.

Camino Easy

Book and cover design by the author.

ISBN: 978-1539676102

CONTENTS

About the Author

B **G Preston is a pseudonym**, I use this simply because my "real name", Barry Sanders, tends to be confused with a noted sports figure in America.

As a retired corporate guy, I have had the pleasure of traveling and exploring much of the globe and doing so in a variety of ways. Trains, planes, automobiles, feet and a few cruise ships here and there.

I have also had the pleasure of writing several novels since retiring. All of my works are intended to provide entertainment and a bit of education along the way. Details on these works may be found in the last section of this book or, look them up on Amazon. The titles are:

- Camino Passages
- Blue Water Bedlam

One of the more enjoyable modes of travel is by foot if done leisurely and with the goal of learning about the scenery and people around you. Yes, sitting back on a cruise ship as you sail past or visit exotic ports of call is wonderful. Driving through new lands and staying in new towns is a pleasure, but the best way to really learn about a place and to really understand it is to do so one step at a time. On foot.

So, it was with each of my Caminos, to be more accurate, the Camino de Santiago. One wonderful step at a time while walking through forests, farmlands, vineyards, along highways, and through towns small and large.

My mantra when traveling is, *"Have fun. Have an adventure. Don't kill yourself."* When it came to preparing for each of my Camino adventures, I always kept this simple mantra in mind.

When planning for my first Camino, the one thing that put me to the test was my tendency to stress over every aspect of the trip. Which "Way" should I travel? How long should I be gone? How far should I go each day? What should I take? When should I go? What if I tire out before the end of a day's scheduled segment. The list of stress-inducing elements continued on.

It turns out, for the most part, the solution was simple. I had just let all of the mass of information and options for doing a Camino get in the way.

As one reviewer of the first edition criticized, most of what is in this small book can be found on the internet. This is 100% true. The difference is that this book is intended to be a simple distillation of the incredible volumes of sometimes contradictory information available on the internet and in the more in-depth guidebooks. The less information you have to consider in making initial decisions, the less stressful your planning will be.

Thus, this book. The Camino should be fun and an adventure. I have learned that little stress needs to be involved if a few simple principles are followed and those principles are outlined here.

I have experienced the Camino by walking alone, walking with friends, and walking with a tour group and each of these experiences helped me to understand how this wonderful trail can be enjoyed by almost anyone.

~ ~ ~ ~ ~ ~

Author's Facebook Page

More information about the author and his publications may be found at:

"www.Facebook.com/BGPreston.author"

Please feel free to use this page to communicate with the author on any questions or suggestions for improvement you may have.

Buen Camino. Now, let's get started.

~ ~ ~ ~ ~ ~

1: Who Should Read This?

Mature audiences only. This work is intended specifically for the "over 50 crowd" and for individuals in this age bracket who are exploring the idea of their first adventure on "The Camino."

The Camino de Santiago is actually a complex set of trails with most of them ending in the beautiful Spanish city of Santiago de Compostela... often referred to simply as "SDC."

This work focuses on the two most popular routes which are typically referred to as "the French Way" or "Camino Frances" and also on the Camino Portuguese/Portugues. Descriptions of other "ways" are not included here.

More critical than the routes described in this volume is who this book is intended for. This is NOT for individuals who are accustomed to long hikes or strenuous outdoor activities.

To put it simply, this book is geared toward individuals

or groups who are curious about this walk and: prefer a few comforts; have little interest in roughing it; and may question their abilities to undertake this adventure.

Why "mature audiences?" The simple answer is that the goals, abilities, and preferences of a younger individual often differ dramatically from those of us who have a few more decades under our belt.

Take this simple quiz:

1. Are you more interested in; (A) stopping to smell the roses, or (B) monitoring your stats on a Fitbit? If you answered "A" – this may be the right book for you.

2. Are you more interested in: (A) enjoying the countryside and the local culture, or (B) putting in as many miles in a day as you can? If you answered "B" – this is not the right book for you. The focus here is to help you enjoy the experience, country, and culture of the Camino, not to finish a marathon.

3. Do you prefer to: (A) Travel lightly and have someone else do the work of moving your stuff from town-to-town, or (B) Enjoy full back-packing and carrying everything with you? This one isn't as critical, but it speaks to a point of view. If you prefer the more athletic approach of full back-packing, while okay, it isn't quite the casual approach that many mature individuals prefer.

If you want to put in as many kilometers per day as possible, camp along the way, and generally like to rough it, this book might not fit your needs.

~ ~ ~ ~ ~ ~

The flow of this book. "Camino Easy" is intended to help the reader with all key decisions. You will first find a list of basic recommendations, followed by an overview of the trails to be considered and then, with these key decision components done, supporting details are provided.

Helpful sites: Throughout the narrative in this book, you will find references to various websites and resources which will help you plan your trip. These are all summarized into one convenient list in the "References" section of this work.

~ ~ ~ ~ ~ ~

2: Some Basic Suggestions

A few high-level recommendations. There are so many options available to someone considering their first Camino that it can be confusing and stress-inducing. To help, listed below are a few simple recommendations. The rationale behind many of these suggestions is in the following chapters.

Note: These suggestions assume you will be walking for your Camino and not taking one of the bus/van tour options. While those "walk-and-ride" options are perfectly fine, they do not fit cleanly into these recommendations. Please see following chapters for comparison of the various options of walking vs. walk-and-ride.

It should be noted that every one of the following suggestions comes with a few variations and caveats. Please see the following chapters for further details.

~ ~ ~ ~ ~ ~

1 – Your "End Point":

Plan your walk to end in "SDC", Santiago de Compostela. For your first (maybe only) Camino do not consider starting further down the trail such as the starting point of the Camino Frances in Saint Jean Pied De Port (SJPDP) in France. The day of the week you arrive in SDC does not matter as the Botafumeiro service is not currently active. (See details further in this book).[1]

2 – Don't "mix-and-match" trail segments:

Some individuals may strive to see "the best of" the Camino by dividing a two-week walk (or longer) into two entirely different areas of one of the popular trails. For example, you might be pondering the wisdom of starting your hike in France at Saint Jean Pied De Port and walking to Pamplona…. then skipping over to Sarria for the second week of your walk.

In short, don't do this. It is not necessary. The segments outlined in this book for both the French Way and the Portuguese Way are all contiguous and each of these walks give you a wonderful variety of experiences and scenery.

---

[1] The Botafumeiro service may be reactivated later in 2020. It is important that you check with the Pilgrim's office website office for updates. Once updates to the cathedral are complete, it is likely this service will reconvene.

3 – Which Trail:

The selection of choosing the "French Way" vs. the "Portuguese Way" is in part based on when you go. Both trails provide a wonderful and varied experience and each trail has its own strengths and weaknesses. This will be detailed further in this work.

If you are traveling during the shoulder Spring or Fall months, both trails offer an enjoyable experience. If traveling during the busy summer months of June/July/August, and you wish to avoid crowds, you should select the Portuguese Way.

Note: As depicted in the charts shown in this work, the Portuguese Way is less hilly, (with a few minor caveats). If you are concerned about your abilities to walk over numerous hilly sections, the Camino Portugues may be more appropriate for you.

4 – When Should You Go:

As cited above, your trail/Camino selection should be predicated on the month you choose to take this trip.

For most individuals undertaking this individual, it is highly recommended that you travel during the shoulder months of either April to early June OR late Sept through October if at all possible.

During the summer months of June, July, August, each trail can become far more crowded, inns and albergues are likely to book up and long lines at meal and toilet stops are frequently found.

During the winter months of November through March, rain in Galicia, (the region of Spain where Santiago de Compostela is located), can be common with substantial snow in the hills. In addition, many services, restaurants and inns shut down during this period.

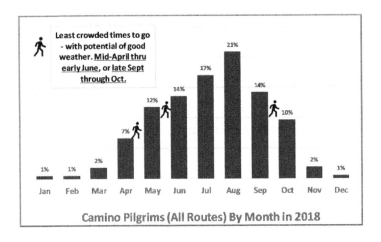

Camino Pilgrims (All Routes) By Month in 2018

5 – Using a Camino Service:

For a one week walk, you should utilize the services of one of the many Camino travel services such as Mac Adventures, Camino Ways, Santiago Ways, and many others.

For a two week walk or longer, you may find it advantageous to do your own booking… details and rationale provided further in this work.

6 – Rest Day:

If planning a 2 week walk, DO plan on building in a rest day mid-way. For the Camino Frances, this should be in Sarria. For the Camino Portugues, this should be in Tui in Spain or Valenca in Portugal.

7 – Luggage Transfer:

Do not plan on carrying a large backpack with you. Plan on only having a midsize daypack with you on the trail. Keep most of your items in a suitcase or larger pack which will be transferred each day. If you use a Camino travel service or make all of your reservations, do build this into your planning.

8 – Detailed Guidebook:

There are several popular and excellent guidebooks to each of the major Camino trails. Acquiring one of these in your early stages of planning can be overwhelming and actually not even provide the basic guidance you need.

The author recommends that you acquire one of the detailed guidebooks AFTER you have decided on the key elements of your trip. Then, while you are on the Camino, a guidebook (only 1 is needed) can be used each evening to study the details on the upcoming days hike.

The most detailed books are authored by John Brierley and details can be found in the reference section of this book.

9 – Extra Day in Santiago de Compostela:

It is helpful and potentially important to have a full extra day in "SDC" at the end of your walk and not plan on flying home after just one night in Santiago. This extra day may be needed to acquire your valuable "Compostela" and provide some tourist time in this delightful area.

10 – Traveling Alone vs. a Tour Group:

If you are traveling by yourself and not with friends or family, do not have worries about undertaking this walk alone. Do consider one of the many structured Camino tours only if you have health concerns or really do not want to start out walking by yourself.

11– Social Media:

Join the Facebook group *"Slow Strollers on the Camino."* This is an excellent source for information and advice geared to individuals who are more inclined to want to take it easy when undertaking this adventure. (Caution, like many social media sites, expect to find some highly biased and snarky responses to your queries).

12– Albergues / Inns / Camping:

If you desire a bit of privacy and a few modest luxuries (such as an actual bed), stay in inns and hotels along the Camino. (This is the option taken by almost every Camino travel service). Most inns or hotels are not expensive.

If you want the "true/rustic" experience, consider having one to many of your nights in the albergues. These are essentially hostels. Less expensive than inns for the simple reason that these are little more than bunk houses.

Do not plan on camping. Camping outdoors is not a common way of spending your nights along the Camino and the availability of campsites can be quite limited.

~ ~ ~ ~ ~ ~

3: The "French Way" vs. the "Portuguese Way"

 Portions of only two "ways" are detailed in this book.

- Camino Frances: The most popular route which starts in the French border town of Saint Jean Pied De Port and finishes in Santiago de Compostela, Spain. (SDC), and...

- Camino Portuguese : The second most popular route with its start in Lisbon, Portugal. Focus is on the "Central route." This path leads from Portugal and, like most "Caminos" finishes in SDC.

Why this limited coverage? As the title of this book states, this is an "Easy" and stress-reducing guide. The two walks detailed here give an enjoyable and varied set of experiences. Other walks, such as the Camino Norte or Portuguese Coastal, are not addressed, but should be considered for a second or later adventure.

To view current statistics on the percent of pilgrims who select the various "Ways" – check out: AmericanPilgrims.org for detailed statistics on Camino travelers. One note of interest, the above-cited "AmericanPilgrims.org" website includes a list of local chapters/groups of individuals who are interested and have experience with the Camino. This may offer the opportunity to meet with others with similar interests. You will also find links to various Camino Facebook pages here, including FB pages geared to the mature hiker.

~ ~ ~ ~ ~ ~

The French Way / Camino Frances

Almost 60% of individuals who walk the Camino de Santiago take the French Way. It should be noted that the other "Ways" are growing in popularity. Some people choose to do the full path, while most opt to walk smaller portions, often for one week.

While this book's focus is on a one-or-two-week adventure, it is just as easy to structure a walk for a much longer period.

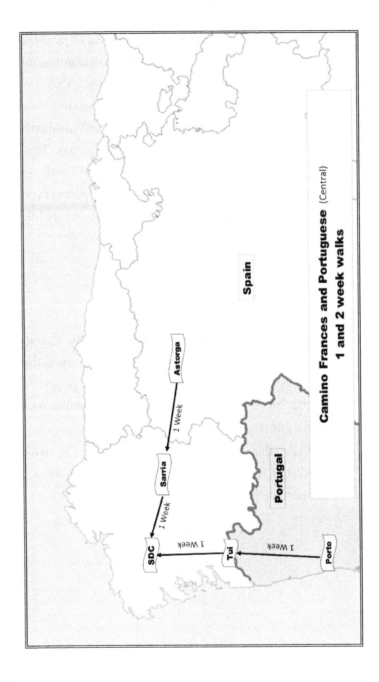

Camino Frances and Portuguese (Central)
1 and 2 week walks

The most popular starting town for shorter walks is in Sarria. This also includes guided groups, most all of which start from here.

Camino Frances Videos

Highly recommended watching. A series of over 30 YOU TUBE videos on the Camino Frances.

"Efren Gonzalez Comino de Santiago"

Select the video(s) most relevant to the trail segments you are interested in.

Examples of suggested starting points:

- 1 week walk – start in Sarria (115 km to SDC)
- 2 week walk – start in Astorga (260 km to SDC)
- Options for starting a longer walk:
  - Leon: (310 km to SDC)
  - Sahagun (368 km to SDC)
  - Burgos (492 km to SDC)
  - Logrono (615 km to SDC)
  - Pamplona (710 km to SDC)
  - The full French Way – starts in Saint Jean Pied de Port in Franc (775 km to SDC). Generally thought of as a 35 to 40 day walk, depending on your abilities and preferences.

Many individuals who walk all of the Camino Frances, do so in segments. If your own abilities or schedule do not enable you to be on the trail for over a month in one stretch, you can easily do this in "chunks" and travel the trail over a period of two or three years. As previously advised, if you are not certain if you will be able to walk the full route then you should start at a mid-point which will enable you to reach Santiago.

Don't worry about missing out on places or experiences of note by focusing strictly on the French Way. You won't. This popular trail offers everything you could want with a rich variety of experiences, historical buildings, villages, and terrain.

The French Way has its official start in Saint-Jean-Pied-de-Port in France and extends for 775km (about 480 miles) as it works its way west to Santiago de Compostela. There are many good starting points to take along the "French Way" as depicted on the prior page.

By selecting the "French Way," you can be certain to have a great set of experiences which will immerse you in the culture. After having experienced all or part of this walk, you might then want to experience the mountainous and more remote "Northern Way", or the historic Portuguese Way.

~ ~ ~ ~ ~ ~

What is "The French Way" like? The answer to this question is it somewhat dependent on which portion you walk:

<u>Sarria to SDC, (the most popular segment)</u>

- Positives:
  - o Generally rolling hills with only two slightly bigger hills to hike over.
  - o Widely varied scenery and terrain.
  - o Substantial number of services available of all types.
  - o An enjoyable variety of villages and towns to visit.
  - o Never any lengthy segments through cities or along highways (until your final few km into SDC)
  - o Often a festive atmosphere.
- Negatives:
  - o Can be crowded during the summer months which can equate to long lines at rest stops for food and toilet.
  - o Many bicyclists on portions of the trail. (Not all of the trail is shared between walkers and bikers).

<u>Astorga to Sarria:</u> (Week 1 of a 2 week hike).

- Positives:
  - o Varied and appealing scenery. (To the author, this was the most scenic and memorable section of the trail encountered along either the French Way or the Portuguese Way).
  - o Opportunity to visit significant historical sites: Templar Castle, O Cebreiro, and Astorga's cathedral.
  - o You will cross the highest point along the Camino at the

Cruz de Ferro.

o   Far less crowded than the Sarria to SDC stretch.

o   Fewer bicyclists than the Sarria to SDC segment.

-   Negatives:

o   This segment has some of the steepest and lengthy hilly hikes on the Camino. This can be either quite enjoyable or overly challenging, depending on your preferences and physical abilities.

o   Long city walks out of Ponferrada and Leon (if you choose to start out of Leon instead of Astorga).

o   Lengthy stretch along a busy highway. (See section on taxis and busses re avoiding this.)

~   ~   ~   ~   ~   ~

Movie Suggestion

For a bit of fun, watch

"The Way"

starring Martin Sheen. This is an enjoyable, inspiring and fictional tale taking place on the French Way with the characters loosely based on *"The Wizard of Oz."*

The Portuguese Way / Camino Portugues

The Portuguese Way is the second most popular trail into Santiago de Compostela and is steadily increasing in popularity. NOTE: The Portuguese Way is often referred to as "Cami<u>nho</u> Portugues" when in Portugal. A completely different spelling.

The full length of this trail is "only" 633 kilometers, starting in Lisbon. In comparison, the full "French Way" is 775 km.

Portuguese Way Video Suggestion

If you are considering the Portuguese Way, watch the YouTube video

"Portuguese Camino de Santiago"

by Karen and Wayne. An excellent video of a mature couple undertaking the walk from Porto to SDC.

Approximately 20% of individuals who walk the Camino de Santiago take the Portuguese Way. This includes the two primary paths of "the Coastal Route" and "the Central Route."

This book focuses on the Central Route for the simple, and biased, opinion that this is more Camino-like instead of the Coastal Route with lengthy portions alongside beaches and the ocean. It should be noted that the two paths do merge at the border of Spain and Portugal.

As a general guideline – build your first trip to end in Santiago de Compostela and work southward from there to determine your starting point based on your available time.

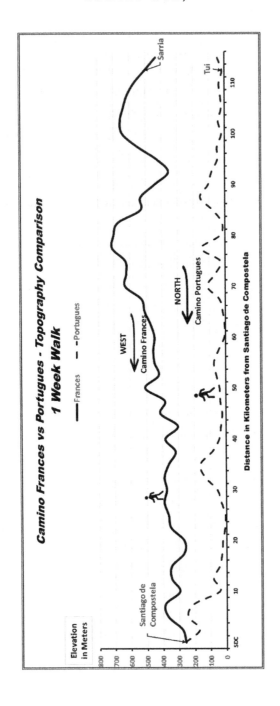

Camino Frances vs Portugues - Topography Comparison
1 Week Walk

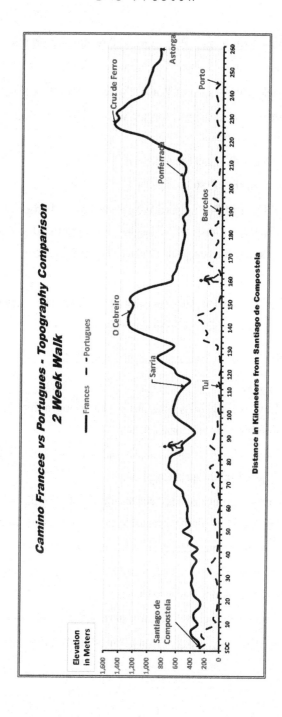

Examples of suggested Portuguese Way starting points:

- 1 week walk – start in Tui, Spain (118 km to SDC)
- 2 week walk – start in Porto, Portugal (248 km to SDC)
- Options for starting a longer walk. (Time involved varies per your ability and preferences)
    - Agueda: (330 km to SDC)
    - Coimbra (380 km to SDC)
    - The full Portuguese Way – starting in Lisbon (633 km to SDC). Generally thought of as a 25 to 30 day walk, depending on your abilities and preferences.)

What is "The Portuguese Way" like? The answer to this question depends on which portion you walk:

Tui, Spain to SDC, (the most popular segment)

- Positives:
    - Low rolling hills and fairly flat topography with no notable climbs along the way.
    - Somewhat varied scenery and terrain. Definitely an enjoyable and relaxing hike.
    - Good number of services available of all types. (Not as prevalent as on the French Way but definitely enough.)
    - An enjoyable variety of villages and towns to visit.
    - Few number of lengthy/unpleasant segments through cities or along highways.
    - Small to no crowds at any part of the year.
    - Fairly easy walk. Many individuals state they are

comfortable in doing the walk in sandals or loafers with no need for heavy hiking shoes.

- Negatives:
  - o Can be quite hot in the summer months.
  - o Not as scenic or historic as the French Way but still a nice variety.

Porto, Portugal: (Week 1 of a 2 week hike).

- Positives:
  - o Varied and appealing scenery.
  - o Only one notable hill to cross over. Highest ascent is approx. 350 meters.
  - o Opportunity to visit the beautiful city of Porto and several notable sights on the route to Tui.
  - o Well-marked trail.
  - o Generally minimal crowds, even in the summer months.

- Negatives:
  - o By far, the biggest negative of the Porto to Tui segment are the cobblestones. There are many lengthy sections of old cobblestone-laden trails and roads which can be very tiring to walk on.
  - o Lengthy industrial/city walk out of Porto. (See chapter on taxis and busses and which sections to avoid.)

SOCIAL MEDIA

Consider joining the Facebook group:

"Caminho Portuguese Pilgrims"

This group is targeted to specific questions and
issues you may have on this trail.

~ ~ ~ ~ ~ ~

4 : Walking for 1 Week

Roughly one third of individuals hiking the Camino do so for just one week. (27% from Sarria and 7% from Tui)

If you are wondering if it is worth it to just walk the final segment into Santiago de Compostela from either Sarria (on the French Way) or Tui (on the Portuguese Way), the answer is a definite yes!

If you wish to receive the Compostela certificate in Santiago de Compostela, Sarria or Tui are the shortest distances you can walk to obtain it.

If your available time is limited, or you are concerned about your capabilities, it is reasonable to wonder if you should bother with just doing the final stretch of a little over 100 kilometers. Again… yes.

Walking from either Sarria or Tui, beautiful small cities in their own right, provides a wonderful array of scenery and experiences. Either of these one week walk allow you to explore many villages and towns, experience varied terrain, and walk through forests and farms.

It should be noted that, with either trail, the walk is fully in the region of Galicia and that region can be quite hilly, this is especially so with the walk from Sarria to SDC.

The only downside, to the French Way stretch from Sarria to SDC, is it can be a bit crowded, especially in summer months. As a result, you will likely find lines at break stops for meals or toilets. One way to reduce the crowd effect is to leave early in the mornings.

A wonderful way to have a holiday which combines the joys of walking the nearly 115km along with exploring this historic area is to stay in Santiago de Compostela for two or three nights at the end of your walk. Use this city as your base camp and then take a variety of day tours.

~ ~ ~ ~ ~ ~

5: **Some Camino Basics**

 Of possible interest some general information about the Camino and who hikes it may be of help.

1 – Number of hikers/pilgrims on the Camino:

Over 300,000 people have received a Compostela certificate in Santiago per year in recent years. The actual count of individuals on the Camino is difficult to count but is steadily on the rise. In 2018, the number was over 330,000.

The difficulty in measuring the number of pilgrims on the trail is due to the situation that many individuals do not reach Santiago and some simply choose to not receive a certificate upon arriving in Santiago. Such individuals will go uncounted as there is no register of individuals do not obtain their Compostela.

Put simply, this is an extremely popular endeavor and the number of people on the Camino is steadily growing but difficult to measure in full.

The volume of hikers may cause you to be concerned about crowds potentially ruining the experience. For the most part, don't let concerns about crowds deter you. Certainly, hiking this trail will be unlike any wilderness hike you may have encountered. The volume of people will rarely be so crowded that it will make the walk unpleasant.

An exception to this rarely crowded statement is for the first portions of the stretch from Sarria during the summer months. Sarria is a common starting point for many tours and groups and most of these groups tend to start around 7:30 AM to 8:30 AM. This combined with an initial uphill stretch can slow many individuals down resulting in a log-jam. After a few kilometers. the crowds will disperse, and you should find yourself having an enjoyable trek.

~ ~ ~ ~ ~ ~

2- Hikers vs. Pilgrims:

The two terms of "hiker" or "pilgrim" are often interchangeable although different in intent. Loosely defined, a "Pilgrim" or "Peregrino" is considered to be an individual who is traveling the Camino for religious reasons. In practice, the term "Pilgrim" is often applied to everyone on the Camino. A "Hiker" is an individual who has chosen to take the Camino for reasons ranging from simple pleasure to adventure seekers, and to those desiring time to walk and reflect.

For simplicity, the term "Pilgrim" will be used throughout this book instead of "Hiker."

Almost 50% of individuals cite that they are traveling the Camino specifically for religious reasons. It is never a problem if you choose to hike for reasons other than religion. Roughly half of the individuals who receive their documents in Santiago cite they are traveling for "other reasons" or "religious and other." This said, it is highly recommended that every person on the Camino, regardless of religion or lack thereof, plan to attend one or more Pilgrim Masses along the way. The trail has deep religious roots and it is only reasonable that you experience a bit of this as part of your adventure.

~ ~ ~ ~ ~ ~

3 – Profile of Hikers and Pilgrims:

The following statistics may help understand the incredible variety of individuals on these trails. In short, regardless of your age, sex or religious preferences, you will fit right in.

- **Age:** Roughly 18% of pilgrims are age 60 or greater. This hike is not geared strictly to younger people.

- **Walk vs. Bicycle:** approx. 94% of pilgrims do the Camino on foot as opposed to bicycling. Bicyclists have a longer minimum requirement to receive their Compostela so they must begin at least in Leon on the

French Way or Porto on the Portuguese Way.

You will find that you will be sharing the trail in some segments with bicyclists. Often, the two groups travel different routes.

- **Nationality:[2]**
  - One of the great joys of hiking the Camino is meeting individuals from many other countries. If you open yourself to meeting others along the way, it is likely you will build international friendships.
  - The most common nationality of Camino Pilgrims is Spain with roughly 44% of pilgrims.
  - The United States is the fourth most common country with roughly 6% of total pilgrims.
  - Other popular countries for pilgrims include:
    - Italy 8%
    - Germany 8%
    - Portugal 4%
    - France 3%
    - U. K. 2%
    - Ireland 2%

---

[2] All figures cited here are from the Camino Pilgrim's Office 2018 report. Figures cited are rounded.

- **Women on the Camino:** There is nearly an equal mix of men and women on the Camino. Recent statistics show almost 50% of individuals on the Camino are female. The social aspect and the fact that this is a relatively safe adventure contribute to this.

- When walking the Camino, you will find many women of all age groups walking the Camino alone or in groups.

- Women do, reasonably so, concern themselves with safety issues which men often do not need to consider. It can be of some comfort for a woman to know that it is generally easy to stay in sight of other pilgrims on the trail thus reducing the chance of being alone.

~ ~ ~ ~ ~ ~

4- What is the trail like:

It is common to want to have a hiking trip which only takes you through pristine forests and beautiful scenery. This is NOT what the Camino is about. If you wish to have a walk which allows you to be mainly in the wilderness, it is advised that you consider one of the many popular wilderness trails in North America, Canada or the U.K.

The Camino is about experiencing a country, and this means not all parts of the walk will be through photo-worthy scenery. When reading online blogs some criticism can be found on the nature of the Camino. This criticism comes from not understanding the purpose of this wonderful, but highly varied walk.

A typical day on the Camino is reminiscent of quote from the movie Forrest Gump, *"Life is like a box of chocolates, you never know what you are going to get."* When walking almost any major section of the Camino, you will experience, walk through and often rest alongside:

- o Beautiful forests
- o Farmlands and vineyards
- o Villages and towns of all sizes
- o Flat lands and rolling hills
- o Steep and rocky trails
- o Rivers and creeks
- o Cattle being herded alongside you
- o Highways
- o Cities and towns

It is these last non-wilderness facets of the walk which can be off-putting at first. Don't let it be. Yes, there are sections along highways or through cities, which are not all that pleasurable, but this is Spain and a goal of this walk is to experience northern Spain and the Galicia region. Plus, truth-be-told, there are ways to avoid the less than stellar parts.

If immersing yourself into a culture and experiencing much that it has to offer is of interest, then the Camino can offer all of this to you and more.

Not a "Walk in the park" either

It is important to note that the path you will take, even the most popular final section from Sarria to Santiago can be a bit rugged in places. This is surprising for a trail which is so well traveled.

Be prepared to walk on moderately rocky and hilly stretches and for some long, uphill stretches. The Camino can be anything from dirt and rocks to gravel, paved sections and even muddy stretches. At times, if it has rained, you will likely find yourself needing to do some creative navigation up along stone walls or cautiously stepping from rock to rock to get through wet and muddy stretches.

On the Portuguese Way, on the stretch from Porto to Tui, you will encounter many lengthy cobblestone sections. While appealing to view, this can be tiring to walk on.

This not-a-walk-in-the-park aspect of the Camino also applies to the fact that you will, at times, need to walk alongside busy roads. Typically, these unpleasant stretches don't last long and soon you will find yourself back in more pleasant surroundings.

~ ~ ~ ~ ~ ~

5 - Think Metric:

Kilometers, meters and centigrade. For most Americans, we think in miles and feet for distance and Fahrenheit for temperature.

Every measure in Spain and Portugal is in the metric system. All references to distance will be in kilometers. All references to elevation will be in meters. Temperatures are always depicted in centigrade.

For quick reference - A few conversion basics are shown below. Take a look at them to get a sense of how measurements vary.

- Distance:
  - o 1 km = .62 miles (a bit under 2/3 of a mile)
  - o 1 mile = 1.6 km (a little over 1½ kilometers)
- Height/Altitude:
  - o 1 meter = 3.28 ft (a little over a yard)
  - o 1 foot = .3 meter (slightly under 1/3 of a meter)
- Temperature:
  - o Celsius temps measure up from 32 degrees Fahrenheit (freezing) with each degree in Celsius equal to approximately 1 ¾ degrees Fahrenheit.
  - o A cool day = 15 degrees (about 59 Fahrenheit)
  - o A warm day = 25 degrees (about 77 Fahrenheit)
  - o A hot day = 30 degrees (about 86 Fahrenheit)

Develop a Metric Mind Set. Try to forget any and all conversion charts, such as the previous one. Learn to speak metric and stop attempting ongoing measurement conversions. This is another way to keep it simple.

For your walk, just look at how many kilometers you will walk each day. If you walked 12 kilometers, that should equal...12km. Don't try to convert it to miles. You are in Spain... use and think their measurements.

When/if you watch any news on TV while in Inns along the way, all references to temperatures will be Celsius. So, as cited above, just remember the general guideline that if the temperature is in the mid-teens, then you have a cool day ahead and if the temperature is over 25 then prepare for a hot day.

If you are using a sports app which measures distances, set it to kilometers. You may even want to do so when you do your prep walks back home so as to help tune into the metric system.

~ ~ ~ ~ ~ ~

6: **Going Alone vs. with a Tour Group**

 There is a mode of travel on the Camino for almost everyone.

> **This may be the most important chapter in this book as it sets the framework for everything else involving your Camino.**

There are a multitude of ways to travel the Camino and this can include everything from doing no pre-planning at all to all-inclusive bus trips which make occasional stops along the Camino.

The term "MY CAMINO" is a critical one. This simply means there are many, many ways to undertake this wonderful journey and there is no one right or proper way. It is your personal way.

If you already have a group of travel companions this may not be relevant to you. If you are undertaking the Camino alone or just with one or two companions, you may be questioning if you should join up with a tour group or do this by yourself.

Most common options for undertaking the Camino include:

- Traveling alone and doing all of the travel arrangements yourself.

- Traveling alone but working with a Camino travel service for them to book many items for you.

- Joining a Camino walking tour group.

- Taking a walk-and-ride van or bus tour.

"My Camino"

A wonderful aspect of the Camino is that it can be structured to fit almost any person's abilities and these varied preferences can and do coexist quite well on this wonderful set of trails.

Notes on Traveling Alone:

If you are concerned about undertaking the Camino by yourself and without any hiking friends, for the most part, don't be worried. Go ahead and, without trepidation, undertake the journey by yourself.

You are rarely alone on the Camino during the months of April through September. There will almost always be another pilgrim near you to exchange information with.

If you do hike alone, you will soon find that you are seeing familiar individuals at meal stops and at monuments along the trail. By the end of your second day, if you are the least bit sociable, you will soon find that you have a steady group of new Camino friends to hike the trail with and meet during dinners.

If you are considering joining one of the many Camino walking tours simply from being concerned about traveling by yourself, don't be. While there are many benefits to these tour groups, doing it solely for not walking alone is unnecessary.

Exception to above: If you have medical issues and are concerned that problems may arise while you are alone, it is advised that you consider joining one of the tour groups. They are generally able to help with most problems such as taking you to a medical clinic or finding an open pharmacy.

~   ~   ~   ~   ~   ~

Going DIY: (When walking alone or with a group of friends).

Doing all of the planning and making reservations yourself. With this method, you will select and book some to all rooms before your walk begins and you will book some luggage transfer should you not be wearing a full backpack.

- Pros: Increased flexibility and reduced costs. (For a walk of 1 week the cost savings is minimal, but this cost advantage increases with longer trips.)

- <u>Cons:</u> You need to do more pre-planning and work. Some hotel stays might not be prepaid before you leave causing you to need cash or a credit card to cover the cost along the route.

- <u>Risk:</u> Potential of not finding a good room in an upcoming town. This risk is low in the spring or fall, and high in the summer.

- <u>Recommendation:</u> If choosing the DIY method, book your first two or three nights of your walk and the last night(s) in Santiago de Compostela before departing. Also book luggage transfer for your first two or three days of walking in advance.

This provides peace of mind knowing that the start and end of your hike are set up while giving you flexibility of where you stay and how long you walk for the majority of your hike. Doing this allows you to travel at the same pace as other Camino friends which you meet along the way.

- <u>Resources:</u> See the resource section near the end of this book for a list of helpful resources for booking nightly stays and luggage transfers.

~ ~ ~ ~ ~ ~

Camino Travel Service:

There are several firms which enable you to purchase a package which includes hotels and luggage service. (Camino Ways, Macs Adventure / Santiago Ways, and others)

These services often include some meals. Pilgrim passport will be provided and, typically, a help desk to provide support during your walk.

In most cases, the firms will also provide substantial material about your walk and what to expect for each day.

Most firms allow you to schedule your Camino to fit your needs and pace your walk according to your preferences.

- Pros: Simple, stress-free mode of travel. All hotels have passed quality criteria. Luggage tags are provided. Custom guidebooks. Trip insurance is typically offered. All hotels, many meals and baggage transfer, are pre-paid before you depart, resulting in fewer items to have to arrange yourself.

- Cons: More expensive than DIY and the walk is more structured with resulting loss in flexibility. (Note: While this is more expensive than doing it yourself, the cost for a week's walk is, for some firms, not bad given all they do for you.)

  If you do utilize a Camino travel service, expect to pay roughly 30% to 50% over booking everything yourself.

- Hotels: All hotels are preselected by the travel service. Several services offer levels of quality ranging from standard rooms to luxury.

- **Recommendation:**
  - ○ <u>One week walk:</u> Utilizing a Camino travel service is strongly recommended for any first time pilgrim wishing to do a one week walk on the Camino, regardless of the trail.

  - ○ <u>Two week walk:</u> Consider using one of these Camino services only if you are uncomfortable with doing it yourself or are fine with the schedule fully locked in for each day of your trip.

  - ○ <u>Three week walk or longer:</u> Highly recommend that you do all booking yourself for the increased flexibility and greatly reduced cost.

~ ~ ~ ~ ~ ~

Guided Group Walks:

If you wish to travel with others in a group and with a guide, a few firms provide this service.

Most guided walks cover only the last 100+km which is the minimum distance to receive your Compostela document upon arrival in SDC.

<u>French Way</u>: Almost all guided walks are for one week and begin in Sarria. 114km. A few guided walks cover the first leg which begins in Saint Jean in France and finishes in Pamplona. See the detailed resource section near the end of

this work for a list of these firms.

<u>Portuguese Way:</u> Most guided walks are for one week and, depending the firm, travel either the Central Route which starts in Tui (118km) or the Coastal Route which begins in Baiona, Portugal (126km)

The role of a guide on these walks is generally not to function as a tour guide who points out and describes points of interest. Their role is typically to provide a morning orientation, ensure everyone's safety, provide support when needed, meet the group at selected mid-points each day, arrange group dinners.

One of the services included with most guided group walks is transportation to your starting point from the airport, a very helpful feature. Most tours, for both the French Way and Portuguese Way, will meet at the Santiago de Compostela airport and then bus to your starting town from there.

Availability of walks with guides can be limited in quantity and the size of the groups will normally be fewer than twenty individuals. These group walks tend to book up quickly.

o   <u>Pros:</u> Walk with a group of like-minded individuals and enjoy their company along the way starting right from your first hour on the Camino. Simple, stress-free way of travel. Availability of a guide should problems arise. Accompanied by an English-speaking guide.

o   <u>Cons:</u> Limited availability of group walks and departure dates. No or minimal flexibility in the schedule. Higher cost than most other modes. Group dinners are held late, often not starting until 8:30 or later in the evening.

o Hotels: All hotels will be selected by the agency and reserved for you. Typically, all guests will stay in the same hotel and join in group dinners which also helps build camaraderie.

o Recommendation: Use this mode of travel if you desire the comfort of walking in a group right from the start and will only be walking from Sarria or Tui.

o Firms to consider: The following are examples of firms which provide guided walks. Check the fee structure closely as the costs for these services can vary dramatically. All of these firms will offer guided walks for the French Way from Sarria. Guided walks for the Portuguese Way are not as common and many of them use the Coastal Route instead of the Central Route recommended in this book.

- CaminoWays.com (Reasonably priced)

- Santiago Ways.com (Reasonably priced)

- FrescoTours.com (Expensive)

- MarlyCamino.com (Expensive)

- Backroads.com (Very expensive)

- To find and evaluate the full list of firms which provide guided walks, do an online search for "Camino de Santiago guided walking tours."

Bus and Walk Tours:

A group Camino tour will take you on a small bus or large van along the Camino. These tours always include a guide.

Tours tend to provide a mix of walking and bus rides and typically tout their tours as "the best of." The walking portions are commonly along the more scenic stretches of the Camino with daily walks of roughly 5 to 8km.

Many of these tours start in Leon or Pamplona for the French way or from Lisbon for the Portuguese Way. This longer distance covered for one week enables you to view more of this region while not having to walk it all.

The tour company will include your hotels and many meals. Luggage service is automatic as your luggage comes along with you on the bus.

Another difference with the bus and walk tours is many of them provide side-tours to historical places of interest which are not directly on the Camino.

o   Pros: Easy mode of travel which almost everyone, at any age or ability, can undertake. See more of the region. For the walking portions, you can choose to remain aboard the bus or van if you are not able to undertake the walk.

o   Cons: Higher cost than all other modes of traveling the Camino. You have little opportunity to walk the trail alone. Group dinners typically are held fairly late by mature/American standards.

o   Hotels: All hotels are booked for you by the travel firm.

o   Recommendation: A great way to view the Camino if you are not certain of your abilities or prefer a more leisurely approach.

o   Firm to consider: Several firms offer combination walk/bus tours. In each case, there are a limited number of tours available. Firms offering Camino walk/bus tours include (and are not limited to):

   o   Camino Ways: Their offerings are fairly typical in that the tours last for 1 week. Each day will include a mix of bus travel and walking.

   o   Follow the Camino: Offerings tend to travel further than many other firms. A common offering from this firm is a full 700km, traveling from Bilbao to Santiago de Compostela. Each day includes a mix of riding and walking.

Again, whether you choose to fully rough it or relax and take the bus remember the important phrase "My Camino." It is your Camino to define as you desire.

~ ~ ~ ~ ~ ~

7 : A Typical Day

While your experiences each day differ, your schedule will be fairly predictable. Understanding a typical Camino day can be helpful and should reduce planning stress.

As shown in the previous chapter, there are many ways to travel the Camino, including walking, bicycling and even bus tours. This chapter assumes you will be walking, which is how more than 90% of pilgrims complete their adventure.

Your Day

- **Get up early and don't shower in the morning.** Showering is for the evening. Just get dressed and you should be ready to go.

  If you shower in the morning, it is almost impossible to get your feet as dry as they need to be. Walking with even slightly damp feet is a great way to get blisters. Just splash some water on your face and hair and you should be ready. For most women, this means forget about makeup… really.

- **Breakfast early and minimally**. Breakfasts on the Camino are typically light with few choices.

    You don't want to start your walk on a very full stomach. Opportunity for a second breakfast or snack will come soon enough. If you are accustomed to having a large glass of juice or cup of coffee in the morning…DON'T. At every stage of your hike, drink and eat in small amounts for the simple reason that you do not know how far the next toilet stop will be.

- **Luggage out of the room early.** If you are using a luggage transfer service (highly recommended), they typically require that your bag is for pick-up by 8:30 AM.

    Placement of your bag in the morning will vary by the inn/alburgue and the manager of each establishment will tell you what to do.

- **Start your walk early.** You will generally want to plan on departing before 8 AM. Many individuals start much earlier which is a great way to get to the first coffee and toilet stop before the crowds.

    One oddity should be noted. Many villages are nestled in valleys which means that to get out of the village in the morning you will likely find yourself walking uphill for the first few kilometers. This is one more reason to not start out on a full stomach.

- **Walk 4 to 6 kilometers** (about 3 miles). Walk an hour or so then get your first coffee and snack for the day.

- **Your average walk will likely be around 20km.** The distance you travel in a day can vary from as few as 10km to as much as 30km. Key variables will be the terrain, your own preferences, and the distance between villages and towns.

  Don't worry about your ability to complete a 20+km stretch for a day. If you are scheduled for a long distance in a day and your feet are telling you otherwise, this won't be a problem. (see section on taxis and busses)

  In many cases, even when working with firms who do all of the booking for you, you will be able to set an itinerary with short segments for almost every day. This will mean that the overall time on the Camino will be longer.

- **Take your time.** Slow hiking is fine. Don't make it a race. If possible, obtain an understanding of your walking speed during preparation walks at home.

  Most individuals hike at a pace somewhere around four kilometers per hour. Your prep walks are likely to depict you walking at a faster pace which is normal. Once you get on the trail and have walked for several days, a steadier and slightly slower pace is likely to set in.

  The author, for example, hiked roughly 5km per hour in prep walks at home, but walked the Camino at a far more leisurely 4km per hour.

- **Expect to take two to four stops each day.** In some ways, these short breaks are the best times on the Camino as you take a moment to sit, relax, chat with others, have a snack and a drink. These snack bars increase in frequency as you get closer to Santiago de Compostela. In the more remote areas, you will rarely be more than 5 or 6 kilometers from an opportunity to rest and get a snack.

  Your stops should include visits to the small churches along the trail to obtain sellos/stamps in your Camino passport. On many occasions, you may simply find a relaxing spot in the shade to sit, relax and watch other pilgrims walk on by.

- **Arrive at your inn or albergue (al burr gay).** Expect to finish your day's travels sometime between 2 PM to 3 PM depending on how long you have walked that day. (See chapter on Hotels and Albergues).

- **Laundry**. First thing after checking in to your hotel, <u>do your laundry</u> and shower. Washing just a couple of items per day is a great way to decrease the volume of items you need to pack. When possible, try to handwash your items.

Do not pack cotton clothing. Bring only easy wicking items including underwear and bras. These items wash and dry easily and do not hold sweat against your body.

While larger establishments do have laundry facilities, they can be very expensive. Doing a few bits of laundry in your room each afternoon will reduce this expense and bother.

- **Siesta.** Many businesses, even the restaurants and bars, in northern Spain, tend to take siestas, and the timing for this is typically from mid-afternoon to as late as 6 PM. You might want to do the same.

  One caution about siesta timing: If you arrive in a village around 3 PM or so, it is common to find that the inn or alburgue you have booked will be closed for siesta and you can't check in. If so, simply find a cool spot to sit, relax and get a drink. Do as the locals do and kick back until the business opens back up.

- **Explore the town.** Every town and village has something unique to offer. Once you have done your laundry and have relaxed for a bit, take some time to explore a local church, park, historical treasure or bar. This exploration should include a visit to the small church as these can be an excellent spot to obtain your required "sellos", Camino stamp.

- **Dinner.** If you are alone or in a small group, dinner can be done as early as 6 PM, rarely earlier. If you are with a larger group and have a group reservation, you will find that dinner might not start until 8 or 9 PM. This is a problem when you know you will be getting up early the next day to start your walk... thus the value of the afternoon siesta. Simply put, dining late in Spain is common.

- **Prepare for next day's walk.** Shower, if you have not already done so, then lay out your gear and clothes for the next morning.

- **Start out again.** Ideally, when the next day begins, you will simply have to pull on the clothes you have set out, splash some water on your face, put your luggage out (if you are shipping luggage) and start your day's trek.

Get up early… eat lightly…walk in short segments…relax and eat frequently…enjoy the sights along the way…arrive mid-day…laundry…siesta…dinner.

Repeat as needed.

~ ~ ~ ~ ~ ~

8: **Itinerary Suggestions**

Detailed example itineraries follow. At risk of stating the obvious, when planning your trip, you need to consider not only how many days you will be on the Camino but your travel time to and from as well.

A trip of just 7 days, including traveling to and from the Camino, should NOT be attempted.
Plan on a minimum of 10 days.

The minimum suggested time is 10 days to cover:

- Travel to your Camino starting point.
- Your Camino walk – generally a minimum of 7 days.
- Time to tour the Santiago de Compostela area at the end of your walk.
- Travel time home.

When crafting an itinerary, the following guidelines should be considered.

Getting There

IF you are traveling from North America, allow two days to get to your starting Camino point from your home city. If coming in from Europe, this can be reduced to just one day.

Important: If you are planning on taking a bus or train to your starting point from your airport arrival, there may or may not be a train which will get you to your destination on the same day your flight arrives in Spain. It is entirely possible that flights and ground transportation will not align well. In extreme situations, you may need to add in a third day of travel to get to the starting town for your walk.

A typical schedule from North America would go something like:

- Day 1: Leave your home airport and begin your overnight flight(s) to Spain or Portugal (depending on your Camino starting point). This typically means a transfer in a major city such as Paris, Amsterdam or Madrid.[3]

- Day 2: Arrive in Europe. Take a train or bus to your Camino starting point. Arrive there mid-day to early evening.

- Day 3: Start your Camino. Four suggested itineraries

---

[3] The author, who is based in the U.S., has found it to be advantageous to book two separate sets of flights. A round-trip into Paris and then a second, and very inexpensive, flight from Paris into SDC or Porto.

follow.[4]

o 1 week on the French Way from Sarria (the most common)

o 2 weeks on the French Way (2 popular starting points of Astorga or Leon)

o 1 week on the Portuguese Way (Focus on the Central way and not on the Coastal Way. Elements of the two can be combined.)

o 2 weeks on the Portuguese Way. (Focus on the Central Way)

---

[4] **Author's ranking/preference of these four sections.**

- Top Ranking: French Way – Sarria to SDC – wonderful variety of scenery and no part of this trek is overly challenging. Just don't do this hike in the summer.

- Second Choice: Portuguese Way – Tui to SDC – easy hike with enjoyable variety of scenery and towns.

- Third Choice: French Way – Astorga to Sarria: By far the most challenging physically, but it offers some wonderful scenery and historical sights.

- Fourth Choice: Portuguese Way – Porto to Tui. Least attractive and varied walk of all four major segments described in this book. And... those cobblestones!

The following itineraries do NOT include travel time to your Camino starting city and travel time home from SDC.

Camino Hiking Day	Start and End Towns	Distance	Notes
	Example 1 Week Itinerary **FRENCH WAY**		
1	Sarria to Portomarin	22km	One notable hill at the start of the hike out of Sarria. Gentle rolling terrain for majority of the day.
2	Portomarin to Palas de Rei	25km	Similar to day 1. A steady climb out of Portomarin, then level and gentle rolling hills from there.
3	Palas de Rei to Melide	14km	Option of combining days 3 and 4 shown here for a full day into Arzua, skipping the stay in Melide. (Not recommended for the intended audience of this book) After the previous two lengthy days, your feet will enjoy the two shorter days. Terrain: there are no major hills from this point and into SDC.

Camino Hiking Day	Start and End Towns	Distance	Notes
Example 1 Week Itinerary *FRENCH WAY*			
4	Melide to Arzua (Option of Rua)	14km	A relaxing and gentle hike. Several villages and small churches to view along the way.
5	Arzua/Rua to Amenal	23/18 km	(18km if you stopped in Rua instead of Arzua the previous evening) Your last full day on the Camino. A fairly lengthy day but most of it is level or gentle hills.
6	Amenal to Santiago de Compostela	14/22 km	(22km if you travel from Rua) A small uphill stretch in the morning followed by an enjoyable day into SDC where you will obtain your Compostela.
7	Santiago	Na	Highly recommended that you stay at least one additional night in SDC to enjoy this wonderful city and area.

~ ~ ~ ~ ~ ~

Camino Hiking Day	Start and End Towns	Distance	Notes
1	Astorga to Rabanal Del Camino	20km	Steady but not arduous uphill walk to the attractive village of Rabanal Del Camino. (Option of starting in Leon, adding 2 hiking days and additional 52km)
2	Rabanal Del Camino to El Acebo.	16km	The day begins with a moderate climb to the highest point on the Camino at Cruz de Ferro, followed by descent to El Acebo.
3	El Acebo to Ponferrada	16km	Steep descent followed by entry into the beautiful city of Ponferrada. Take time to visit the Templar Castle.
4	Ponferrada to Villafranca del Bierzo	24km	The day begins with a long stretch through Ponferrada (which can easily be avoided via taxi) then a thoroughly enjoyable stretch through wine country as you make your way into the beautiful town of Villafranca del Bierzo.

Example 2 Week Itinerary
FRENCH WAY

Camino Hiking Day	Start and End Towns	Distance	Notes
Example 2 Week Itinerary **FRENCH WAY**			
5	Villafranca to O Cebreiro	30 km	Suggest you start the day with a taxi ride to Vega de Valcarce – to cut the day in half. This first stretch is largely along a highway which is unappealing. From Vega de Valcarce, the climb up to O Cebreiro will either be one of your best or your worst days on the Camino, depending on your abilities. It is a very steep ascent, but the scenery and trail are a delight.
6	O Cebreiro to Triacastela	21 km	A delightful but challenging downhill walk with wonderful views. Very steep in some places which will be a challenge to some.
7	Triacastela to Sarria	19km	Delightful days walk over rolling hills and forested sections.
8	Sarria	Na	Recommended rest day. Sarria is a large town with a lot to see and plenty of opportunities to stock up as needed.

Example *2 **Week** Itinerary* FRENCH WAY			
Camino Hiking Day	*Start and End Towns*	*Distance*	*Notes*
Days 9 to 15			Travel from Sarria to Santiago de Compostela as outlined in the previous chart for a 1 week walk. PLUS – highly recommended to add at one tourist day at the end of your Camino.

~ ~ ~ ~ ~ ~

Example *1 Week* Itinerary
PORTUGUESE WAY

Camino Hiking Day	Start and End Towns	Distance	Notes
1	Tui, Spain to O Porrino	18km	Option of starting in Valenca, Portugal – a town which is across the river from Tui. Some industrial and highway sections along the way. Some of this can be avoided by following the alternate path which is slightly longer but more scenic. (This won't be your most memorable or scenic hiking day.)
2	O Porrino to Arcade	24km	Much of the day will be on streets and pavement. Some moderate climbs.
3	Arcade to Pontevedra	12km	Your shortest and easiest day of walking. Gentle rolling hills. You will be glad you have time on your hands after the walk as Pontevedra is a delightful city to explore.
4	Pontevedra to Caldas de Reis	21km	A relaxing and level hike. Some segments along highways.

Example *1 Week* Itinerary
PORTUGUESE WAY

Camino Hiking Day	Start and End Towns	Distance	Notes
5	Caldas de Reis to Padron	18km	Your last full day on the Camino. Much of the day will be spent traversing up and over a moderate hill.
6	Padron to Santiago de Compostela	25km	A steady uphill hike from Padron into SDC, ending in a city walk for the last several km. Note: some individuals split this day into 2 short days with an overnight stay in Teo. Doing so enables you to arrive early at the Pilgrims Office in SDC to collect your Compostela.
7	Santiago	na	Highly recommended that you stay at least one additional night in SDC to enjoy this wonderful city and area.

~ ~ ~ ~ ~ ~

Camino Hiking Day	Start and End Towns	Distance	Notes
Example 2 Week Itinerary *PORTUGUESE WAY*			
1	Porto, Portugal to Fajozes	25km	City walking for the first part of the day. Suggest you bypass this by taking a taxi the first portion to Maia, leaving a shorter day walking level ground and making for a relaxing first day.
2	Fajozes to Arcos	13km	This short day can be combined with the next day's walk to Barcelos. This does make for a long stretch but none of it is over difficult terrain. (Except for some lengthy cobblestone stretches.)
3	Arcos to Barcelos	20km	An easy day with no major hills to hike across. Arrive early in the beautiful town of Barcelos and do some exploring.
4	Barcelos to Ponte de Lima	34km	A long day which may be split with a night in Balugaes if you prefer or start your day with a short taxi ride to reduce the amount of time on your feet.

Camino Hiking Day	Start and End Towns	Distance	Notes
Example 2 Week Itinerary		
PORTUGUESE WAY		
5	Ponte de Lima to Rubiaes	18 km	A fairly challenging stretch as it includes a 400+meter climb to the highest point on the walk from Porto to SDC. Views from the crest are a great reward.
6	Rubiaes to Tui	20 km	Start the day with a fairly steep downhill section followed by rolling hills until you reach the border with Spain. Option of staying the night in the Portuguese town of Valenca instead of Tui, Spain.
7	Tui or Valenca	Na	Recommended rest day. Time to relax, explore and stock up on supplies.
Days 8 to 14	Travel from Tui to Santiago de Compostela as outlined in the previous chart for a 1 week walk. PLUS – highly recommended to add at one tourist day at the end of your Camino.		

~ ~ ~ ~ ~ ~

9 : Travel to & from the Camino

You may be wondering how you get to the town where you will start your Camino. Following is a set of recommendations for each of the four recommended starting points outlined in the previous itineraries for one-or two-week walks on either the French Way or Portuguese Way.

Don't limit your travel plans to flying

When traveling in Europe you will quickly learn that the train and bus systems are excellent and should always be considered when planning travel.

You will find listings of suggested travel sites in the reference chapter near the end of this book.

General notes for North Americans on flying to your starting point for the Camino:

- Plan on flying into a major airport of Paris or Madrid and then finishing your travels to your starting town from there.

- Consider booking two separate sets of tickets: one from an overnight flight from your home in North America to Paris or Madrid, and the second set of tickets within Europe should be purchased separately. Doing so can be substantially cheaper and, at the very least, provide more flexibility.

- What city to fly into:

Way	Starting City	Fly Into
French Way	Sarria	Santiago de Compostela or A Coruna
	Astorga	Santiago de Compostela or Madrid
	Leon	Madrid
Portuguese Way	Tui	Santiago de Compostela or Porto
	Porto	Porto

~ ~ ~ ~ ~ ~

Ground Travel to Sarria:[5]

Curiously, with Sarria being one of the most popular starting points for Camino pilgrims, it actually is one of the more difficult starting points to reach due to its fairly small size.

- **From Madrid**: While Sarria can be reached via ground travel from the Madrid airport, this is generally not advised due to the 515km distance and lengthy travel time for trains or busses (generally, 6 to 8 hours).

- **From Santiago de Compostela:** You have numerous ground options from SDC to Sarria. It is critical to watch the schedules as departures can be limited.[6]

  Train: Typically, 4 departures a day. Note, you must first take a taxi from the SDC airport to the train station. About 18km. Upon arrival in Sarria, there is a moderate walk, or short taxi ride, to your starting hotel.

  Bus: Typically, 3 or departures per day directly from the SDC airport. A change in Curtis or Lugo is likely.

  Taxi/Town Car: **RECOMMENDED**. By far the most convenient, but also the most expensive. Take a town car

---

[5] Ground Schedules: Recommend use of "Rome2Rio.com" to obtain schedules for most modes of transportation.

[6] Note re structured Camino Group: If you will be joining a walking group, such as those provided by Camino Ways, it is likely that transportation to Sarria from the SDC airport will be provided.

or taxi directly from the SDC airport to Sarria. Cost is higher, but given the convenience, it tends to be worth it if your budget allows. Check out TaxiGalicia.com for rates. Expect costs for a car with 1 or 2 individuals to range between 100 to 150 Euros plus tip.

- **From A Coruna:** Options and availability of ground transportation from here to Sarria are similar to traveling from SDC. The distances and travel times are very close. Consider A Coruna only if (a) you can find better flights into this city over SDC or, (b) you are taking a ferry into A Coruna from the UK or France.

~ ~ ~ ~ ~ ~

Ground Travel to Astorga:

To travel to Astorga for a two week hike on the French Way, you may fly into either Madrid, or Santiago de Compostela.

Generally, you will find it to be advantageous to fly to Madrid due to the increased number of ground travel options available. (Note: Madrid is roughly 100km further from Astorga than Santiago, but travel time can be less from Madrid).

Train: Generally, not recommended due to limited availability. Check the schedule with Rome2Rio.com just in case one of few trains fits your schedule. If available, you may take the train directly from the Madrid airport and change in central Madrid. If traveling from Santiago de Compostela via train, you will find only 1 or 2 trains available per day. You will need to take a taxi or bus from the SDC airport to the train station in Santiago before heading out to Astorga.

Busses: **Recommended** In most cases, you will find taking a bus (either from SDC airport or from Madrid) to be the most advantageous and least expensive way to travel and you will be able to do so directly from your arrival airport. The primary advantage in taking a bus is they travel the route several times a day.

Travel time:

o Bus from Madrid airport to Astorga: Departs 5 times daily for a 4 ½ to 5 hour trip.

o Bus from SDC airport to Astorga: Departs 4 times daily for a 5 to 6 hour trip.

Taxis/town cars: **Worth exploring**, but beware that it can be expensive. This is definitely more expensive than a bus or train. Check out TaxiGalicia.com or GetTransfer.com for costs. Expect to pay over 200 Euros plus tip.

If the cost is not out of range, this is the most convenient and shortest method of travel to your Camino starting point.

~ ~ ~ ~ ~ ~

Ground Travel to Tui:

Tui is situated midway between Porto, Portugal and Santiago de Compostela, so the costs and travel options are similar. (Santiago de Compostela is slightly further from Tui than Porto)

<u>Flying into Porto:</u> One of the biggest savings in travel time may be to fly into Porto instead of Santiago de Compostela. Check flight schedules to Porto and SDC from your main arrival city in Europe such as Paris or Madrid. It is likely that you will find more available non-stop flights into Porto than you will if flying into SDC. Most flights into SDC from major gateways require a change of planes which can add time and hassle.

<u>Getting to Tui from Porto:</u>

-   <u>Your most affordable and generally workable option</u> is to take a bus from Porto to central Tui. Several busses travel each day and it is likely you will be able to find one which matches up fairly well with your arrival flight. Note, there are more options available from central Porto than there are from the Porto airport.

-   <u>Your most convenient option,</u> but a bit more expensive, is a private car. This has the significant advantage of taking you directly from the airport to your hotel in Tui. Costs are likely to be in the range of 140 to 200 Euros. A bit pricey, but the convenience may be worth it.

Train is generally not recommended due to limited number of departures each day.

<u>Getting to Tui from SDC:</u>

Buses are generally recommended due to the low cost and general availability. The situation here is very similar to traveling to Tui from Porto. Several busses are available each day, either from the Santiago de Compostela airport, or from central Santiago. Travel time is a bit over two hours.

Town cars or taxis can be expensive to Tui from Santiago than from Porto because of slightly greater distance. Travel time is a little over one hour, but you are taken directly to your hotel and not to a central bus station.

For all destinations – check the Reference section near the end of this book for a listing of travel websites for ground transportation.

~ ~ ~ ~ ~ ~

Ground Travel within Porto:

Starting your Camino in Porto has the tremendous, and unusual, advantage that your Camino departure town is likely to be the same town you fly into. When starting your Camino from Porto, in almost every case you will be able to simply take a bus or taxi directly from the airport to your hotel in the Porto area.

~ ~ ~ ~ ~ ~

Travel Home for both the French and Portuguese Ways:

Most travelers will leave Santiago de Compostela by air. If you wish to extend your trip to explore other parts of Spain or Portugal, many trains and buses are available out of Santiago de Compostela. You could, for example, easily tack on a train trip to Madrid, Lisbon or Barcelona and then leave for home from there.

The Santiago airport is a short taxi or bus ride from the city and is not expensive. As a point of interest, when walking the French Way, you actually walk around the base of this airport during your last day on the Camino.

~ ~ ~ ~ ~ ~

10 : **Hotels, Inns & Albergues**

🚶 **You will experience a variety of lodging on the Camino.** Along the Camino, you can choose any option from sleeping on a bunkbed in a room with dozens of others to selecting luxury accommodations.

Whatever your preference, you will find the majority of lodging to be clean, affordable and convenient. Almost every lodging option you might select will be immediately on or very close to the Camino. There is little worry of having to stray far from the path to find your room for the night.

Camping

True camping, sleeping in a tent and in a sleeping bag, out under the stars is NOT a common thing on the Camino. You can do it, but camping sites are few and, given the low cost of lodging, there is little reason to do so.

This also means that, unlike hiking along a wilderness trail in North America, there is no need for you to bring your own sleeping bag. (Exception, some albergues only provide a bunk and it is up to you to bring a lightweight bag or sleeping bag liner. While this can be a bit of a burden, it is also a great way to avoid bed bugs.)

Inn vs. Albergue Recommendation:

Unless you are looking for a room which will be shared with others, even dozens of others, while you sleep in a bunkbed, stay with inns and hotels and stay away from albergues.

Most of the inns are not expensive and will provide a greater level of privacy and comfort.

Inns instead of albergues?

Some individuals will reject the notion of bypassing albergues as they feel this offers the true Camino experience.

The author does not agree.

If you are using a Camino travel service, it is highly likely that you will be staying in inns and hotels, so the thought of staying in albergues is not relevant.

If you are going DIY where you do all of the booking yourself, you might consider staying one or two nights in an albergue just so you have obtained the experience. (Then head off to a hotel the next night where you can shower and change clothes in private.)

Note: Several albergues are combined with small hotel

units and offer a few private rooms. If seeking a private room, do not immediately shy away from lodging simply because they use the name, "albergue." Many locations now have websites, or can be booked through travel sites, and it is easy to determine the variety of sleeping options available.

~ ~ ~ ~ ~ ~

Albergue and Inn Directory

Several online directories to Camino lodging for albergues, inns and hotels are available. One of the better lists may be found at:

"www.WisePilgrim.com"

Click on the Accommodation Directory, for the trail and segment you will be hiking.

Albergue: (Al burr gay)

- Description: The term "albergue" generally applies to the hostel-like accommodations which are unique to the Camino. Most albergues consist of one or more large rooms which accommodate a large number of guests, typically in bunkbed style. These accommodations are often unisex and many also have shared bath facilities.

    Several types of albergues are available. Some are provided by the local community, others by the church, and many are privately owned.

With the growing popularity of the Camino, the number and variety of these establishments has grown substantially.

- Reservations: Many albergues do not take reservations and operate on a first-come, first-served basis. In the shoulder Spring or Fall seasons, this is generally not a problem. During the more popular Summer season, you do run the risk of not being able to find a bed in your first or second choice albergue.

  o Many guidebooks, including those cited in the reference section of this book, provide detailed lists of albergues and their contact information.

- A "trick" for the high season: If you are hiking during the period of mid-June to early-September, it is not uncommon for albergues in the most common stayover towns to book up. So, look for albergues in the "in between" villages. Many small villages which you tend to pass by have small albergues and they do not book up nearly as quickly as they do in larger towns.

- Albergue pros and cons: The biggest positives to staying in an albergue is the low cost and the likelihood of building friendships with others. The biggest negatives are sharing a room with others and the loss of privacy along with quiet.

A common caution with alberques is the need for earplugs. Do understand that European "body modesty" is not the same as in North America so it is common to be in a room while others of both sexes are changing clothes.

Inns and Hotels:

- Description: A wonderful aspect of the many B&Bs, inns, and hotels along the Camino is the variety you will encounter. As you work your way from village to town, you will have stays in small and ancient inns, country B&Bs, and even larger hotels. In almost every case, you will find that they offer an enjoyable night's stay and many also provide full meal service.

  Luxury hotels are available in the larger towns but, with the exception of Santiago de Compostela or Porto, are generally not recommended. Staying in the top-end hotels will likely remove you from easily being able to share meals and talks with your fellow pilgrims after a long day's trek.

- Santiago de Compostela: Staying in this beautiful city is, and should be, different from all of the stays along the Camino. You have finished your trek, so think about rewarding yourself with a night or two in one of the better hotels, if your budget will allow. Keep in mind that Spain is generally not expensive so even the better hotels will not set you back as much as you would experience in North America.

  A list of suggested hotels for Santiago de Compostela may be found in chapter titled "Arriving in Santiago."

- Reservations: Making hotel reservations is not needed if you select a Camino travel service as they will do this for you.

- If you have opted to book your stays yourself, you will find that most inns and hotels will accept reservations in advance but not all. Sites such as TripAdvisor.com or Booking.com are great ways to research available inns and hotels along the Camino. Also, if you purchase a detailed guidebook, you will find listings of suggested hotels which will include contact information.

Meals at your lodging:

Most hotels, inns, and albergues provide breakfast. Some will also provide dinner. If you utilize the services of a Camino trip planning service, they will generally include breakfast within their fees, and some will include dinner as well. The variety of breakfast foods and drinks is often limited, resulting in small meals. This turns out to be good as you typically will want to eat minimally before starting your day's trek.

Wi-Fi Availability:

Most inns will provide Wi-Fi (pronounced "wee-fee") at no additional charge. This cannot be counted on, however, so be careful not to promise relatives at home that you will "facetime" them every evening. In some situations, this simply won't work. In addition, the quality of the provided Wi-Fi can be weak. The good news is that you will have access to Wi-Fi frequently.

~ ~ ~ ~ ~ ~

11: Luggage Transfer vs. Backpack

You don't need to carry it all on your back.

One of the wonderful things about the Camino is you can choose to either carry a full backpack with all of your belongings, or a small daypack in which you place a limited number of emergency and essential items.

Unless you like carrying heavy loads...

DO consider using one of the many luggage transfer services. They are reliable, affordable, easy to arrange and safe. You can use these services for full backpacks in addition to normal luggage.

When using a daypack, you will pack the majority of your belongings into luggage which a service then moves to your next lodging for you each day.

Not having to wear a full backpack can greatly increase the pleasure of your walk each day and, for many of us, increase the distance you can travel comfortably.

A quick caution. You will need to know where to have your luggage sent each day so, by extension, need to have a reservation at an inn or albergue for the upcoming evening. If you are planning on getting a room "when the mood strikes", then it is best that you use a full backpack and not a luggage transfer service.

Luggage Transfer Service:

Many luggage transfer services exist on the Camino and there should be little to no stress in setting this up.

Included with Camino travel service. If you have chosen to use a Camino travel service/packager (e.g.: Camino Ways, Macs Adventure, etc/), they will set this up in advance for you and it is one less thing for you to have to worry about. With these firms, the cost is included in their base fee.

Luggage tags: When using a Camino travel service, you will be provided with luggage tags specific to you and your agenda. If you are going DIY, you will need to improvise and place a tag on your luggage which states the inn/albergue where your luggage is to be sent.

Reserving while en route: If you are going DIY and not using a pre-paid package, you can typically reserve luggage transfer while at your lodging, the evening before the next day's walk is to begin.

Luggage out Early:

Generally, your suitcase must be out of your room and ready for pick-up by 8:30AM. Placement of your bag will differ for each hotel and Albergue. Some locations will ask that you simply place the bag in the hall outside of your room, most will request that you place your bag in a designated space in the lobby.

Cost:

If you are hiring a service yourself, expect the cost to range between 6 to 10 Euro per suitcase/bag per day. This fee is always paid upfront and not at the point of delivery.

Shipping Backpacks:

You are not limited to using a transfer service just for suitcases. You may also ask the service to ship your backpack from town-to-town providing backpackers with an extra level of flexibility.

Distance Limitation:

Most transfer services will not transfer bags further than 25 or 30 km per day. There are a few exceptions in cases when the distance between usual overnight stops is slightly greater than this.

Avoid Large Suitcases:

Strive to keep your suitcase down in size and weight. There are multiple advantages to this:

• Some luggage transfer services have a weight limitation.

• Many inns and hotels do not have elevators and it can be

unpleasant to have to drag a heavy suitcase up several flights of narrow stairs.

- If you are traveling by train, the amount of space available for larger bags on the train cars can be limited.

Online Luggage Transfer Reservations:

If you are not using a Camino travel service (trip packager) and wish to set this up prior to (or during) your trip, following are example service companies you may wish to consider one of the following:

- Caminofacil.net.
- Jaco Trans; JacoTrans.com
- Bouricot Express; ExpressBourricot.com. This firm also does passenger and bicycle transport in several locations.
- Taxi Belorado; TaxiBelorado.com

The above cites only four resources and, if you wish to book on a day-by-day basis, it is best to use the service recommended each evening by the front desk at your lodging.

Recommendation:

If you are not using a Camino travel service (trip packager), consider booking luggage transfer only the first two or three days in advance. After this, you will better understand your own pacing and you, or someone at each hotel, can reserve the next day's transfer as needed.

Luggage Tags:

At a minimum, you will want to have a tag which cites your name clearly and the destination hotel/albergue. Your phone number can also be of assistance should the transfer company run into any issues.

Recommendation: To be on the safe side, consider writing out a fresh luggage tag each day and placing it in a clear plastic tag holder. (available from Amazon). On this tag, you should write: (a) name of the transfer service, (b) your name, (c) destination hotel and town.

Luggage Security:

In general, these services are safe, and you can count of your luggage arriving at each day's lodging without problems. BUT, for basic security, you should not put any of the following in any luggage which is due to be shipped:

- Passport
- Money
- Wallet
- Jewelry
- Cellphones
- Cameras

~ ~ ~ ~ ~ ~

12: Taxis and Buses on the Camino

Taxis and buses are often available when needed. When looking at a travel itinerary, you might find that some long-distance days are ahead of you. For a mature walker, it would be common to be concerned about your ability to finish a stretch of more than 20km or those sections of trail over steep hills, such as the 28km walk up to O Cebreiro from Villafranca del Bierzo.

The answer is simple. Take a taxi or a bus when needed to make your day a bit easier. There is absolutely nothing to be ashamed of. This is, after all, "your Camino" and you will definitely not be the first person to mix and match walking with riding.

Taxi use along the Camino is common and affordable, however, they are not always immediately available. If you find a need during a day's walk to finish it by taking a taxi or bus, simply ask the staff at the next bar or restaurant you come to. In most cases, they will be able to help you out.

Be prepared to wait a while. Many smaller villages may have limited taxi or bus service, so waiting an hour or two is a possibility. This shouldn't be a problem, especially if you have found a nice place to relax and chat with others.

Avoid the "yucky bits." At times, the Camino sticks to busy highways or takes you through large towns or industrial sections. A wonderful way to enhance your days walk is to be aware of these stretches beforehand, so you can schedule a taxi to the more attractive parts of the trail.

This is where detailed guidebooks can really pay off.

Bring a detailed guidebook with you and each evening study the trail segment ahead of you the next day. Doing this will let you know if reserving a taxi for a portion of the upcoming days walk will be beneficial.

Pass by the sections which may be difficult for you. Some stretches, while attractive and enjoyable to hike, may be more than some hikers should undertake. Quality guidebooks will almost always provide detailed topography maps. From this, you can determine if a short distance taxi ride may be in order.

Where and how to reserve a taxi: You will not need any sort of app or website for this (unless you are the type who can't avoid doing so). Almost every inn/albergue or bar will have taxi information, and many will happily make a reservation for you.

Don't be embarrassed if you want or need to reserve

ground transportation to skip over some sections of the trail. This is a common practice.

Examples of stretches to skip over via taxi or bus:

- **French Way:**
  - o <u>El Cebo to Ponferrada</u> – This is only a 16km stretch although most of it is downhill and can be difficult for some individuals. This is a beautiful stretch, but going downhill can be nearly as difficult as walking uphill. Consider taking a cab for just part of this day's walk if you are concerned about your abilities.

  - o <u>Leaving Ponferrada</u>. It is common to have a schedule of 24km to Villafranca del Bierzo. There are no major hills on this stretch, but it is a fairly long walk to the Ponferrada city limits. Consider taking a taxi in the morning from your hotel to the edge of town near the highway and start your walk from there.

  - o <u>Villafranca del Bierzo to O Cebriero.</u> This long almost 30km stretch has some of the best and the worst of the Camino and both of these warrant review before undertaking this day's walk.

    - ▪ The first ten to twelve kilometers out of Villafranca are often along a busy highway. To enhance your days walk, consider taking a taxi into Vega de Valcarce from Villafranca del Bierzo.

- The stretch from Vega de Valcarce is, for many, one of the most enjoyable and scenic hikes along the Camino. The issue is that there is a lengthy and very steep hill all of the way up to O Cebriero. DO undertake this walk if you possibly can but know that many individuals have to skip it because of the difficulty.

Fun fact – You can take a horse!

Horse rides are often available up to O Cebriero from Las Herrrerias at the base of the mountain. It may not be very comfortable, but it is a fun way to do this otherwise difficult stretch.

- **Portuguese Way:**
  - Porto to Fajozes – The first half of this 25km stretch is through city and along busy streets. Consider taking a taxi or bus to Maia and starting your walk from there.
  - Ponte de Lima to Rubiaes – This stretch takes you over a 400 meter hill. It is an attractive and recommended walk but may be avoided if you are concerned about your abilities to walk this hill.

~ ~ ~ ~ ~ ~

13 : **M o n e y   M a t t e r s**

Euros are absolutely needed on the Camino. In North America and Europe, it is common to use debit and credit cards for most, if not all, purchases. This is not the case on the Camino. Cash is often requested or required.

> ## *Cash is king on the Camino!*

You will find that cash is needed, both paper and coins, at most meal stops and many small stores along the way. Plan on it. Have cash on hand and don't plan on finding cash machines (ATMs) when you need them. ATMs are fairly easy to find in most larger towns but not in many villages.

Most hotels will accept credit cards. Be advised that some of the smaller inns do not.

Recommended Daily Euro Allowance

- IF: You have prepaid your room and dinners through a Camino agency: A daily allowance of 25 to 30 Euros per person per day will cover most needs. (not counting souvenirs).

- IF: You are paying for all rooms and meals along the way, AND, if you are staying in inns/hotels and not albergues – the allowance is far more difficult to judge in advance due to the substantial variance in costs for lodging.

  At a minimum, allow for a full daily cost of 60 Euros per day if you are paying costs for inns and all meals along the way. This can be much higher, depending on your preferences. (Note: if you choose to stay in albergues and not inns/hotels, the daily cash requirement is substantially less.)

  The above variable for lodging, which generates some uncertainty and stress, is one reason for booking inns in most larger towns and cities prior to your embarking on this adventure.

Cash Management and Security:

- How much you should carry: Have at least four days of cash on you as you often will not able to encounter ATMs (or ATMs with available funds) when you need them. This allows for unexpected costs along the way.

- Distribute your cash: For security purposes, divide your cash and keep it in different locations on you. Keep some in a neck or belt wallet, some in an enclosed or zippered pants pocket, and maybe even a few Euros in your daypack.

A few locations ask for (but don't require) a donation of a Euro for the Camino stamps. Some bars ask that you leave a small amount for using the toilet if you are not a customer so have a supply of coins handy. In these cases, you will want immediate access to Euro coins.

While tipping in Spain is far less than in North America, having a stash of Euro coins on hand for tipping is always a good idea.

Euros are the currency of Europe and most unused Euros may easily be spent in other European countries or exchanged at the airport before your return.

Acquire a Starter Supply of Euros Before You Leave

While the best rate of exchange can typically be found in Europe via an ATM, it is still advisable to obtain a small supply of Euros before your walk begins. This may be done at a local bank near where you live, online, or at a currency exchange in the airport.

Your starter kit of Euros does not need to be large, only 250 to 300 Euros. Having this amount on you before you leave removes one more stress point and is one less thing you have to do upon arriving in Spain.

You should have at least two different cards that will work in ATMs to acquire Euros, in case one is stolen/lost or for some reason you encounter problems with an account. Do not keep both/all of your cash cards in the same location such as a wallet. Just as you do with cash, keep one in a neck or belt wallet and the other in a pants-zipper pocket.

For security purposes, consider acquiring a limited-use debit card(s) that is not connected to any of your home accounts. Leave all or most of your usual credit cards at home. Do be careful when doing this and make sure the card will work in Europe.[7]

Don't count on acquiring Euros when you arrive at an airport in Europe. Currency exchange kiosks are generally available in most major airports. This can be problematic as they are not always convenient to where you arrive and pick up your luggage.

Don't wait until arriving in Europe to obtain your starter supply of Euros. You may not have convenient time when you arrive to convert cash. Once you leave your plane, you are working through customs, gathering your baggage, and then are confronted with finding your ground transportation.

~ ~ ~ ~ ~ ~

---

[7] Note re making sure your card will work in Europe. The author, during a recent trip to Europe, had acquired an American express "Serve" card to be used to obtain cash, etc. Upon arrival in Europe, he discovered that the card would not work in Europe... only in the U.S. and Canada. So, just because the firm providing the card is international, such as American Express, do not assume their cash cards will work internationally as well.

14: Social Aspects and Simple Pleasures

You are rarely alone on the Camino. If you choose to walk the Camino at any time from April through October, there is a high probability you will be within sight of other pilgrims. Sometimes, many other pilgrims.

If you choose to be by yourself and not share your experiences with others, you will absolutely be able to do so. Many pilgrims do the Camino with a spiritual or self-awareness goal in mind. If you choose the quiet and solo path, other walkers will almost always honor this.

Even when going alone, you usually have the opportunity to meet other people. Sometimes your visits will last just for a few moments, and other times you can build enduring friendships. This proximity to other pilgrims is one of the great aspects of the Camino.

Many blogs and social media sites cite the value of doing the Camino alone and there is something to be said about this. Even when walking alone, the occasional company of others can be beneficial, educational, and personally rewarding.

"Buen Camino":

You will hear this common welcome from others who are traveling the Camino and even from locals as you pass them on the street. Share the welcome and return the simple greeting, *"Buen Camino."*

Buen Camino literally means "Good Path."

As you walk the Camino, you will find you are soon socializing with individuals from all over the world. This brings up the quirk and limitation of using the term "Buen Camino." When saying this to others, and they respond in kind, you simply do not know if they are also English speakers.

Consider this simple trick, *"Buen Camino and good morning."* These simple few extra words will apprise others that you are an English speaker and greatly increase the possibility of opening a conversation. Adding this extra bit will never be frowned upon.

Exchanging Information:

Sharing information with others along the trail is common and almost expected, but don't force it on others if they seem unreceptive.

> ## The 2 most common questions you will hear on the Camino:
>
> *"Where are you from?"*
>
> And
>
> *"Where did you start your Camino?"*

Most individuals will gladly share basic information and will likely desire the same information from you.

Don't worry if you have walked for only a day or so and you meet up with others who have been walking for weeks. That is the way of the Camino and there are many starting points. There is frequently some pride exuded by those who have walked a great distance, but there is rarely any sense of superiority from a long-distance walker toward a newbie. If anything, the experienced walker may get some joy out of sharing their experiences and advice with you.

Share a Table:

In North America, we are not accustomed to sharing a table in a restaurant or coffee shop with strangers. We tend to want to have our own personal space. On the Camino, this can change as you will often have the opportunity to sit with others when you stop for meal breaks or even at dinner time. Don't pass up the opportunity!

When you come into a full restaurant/café/bar, it is common and accepted for you to ask others if you can share a table with them. Chances are your request will be happily accepted.

When you are having a meal by yourself and see others, and you have a sense that they share your language, offer to share your table.

By sharing your dining space, you can be assured to make many new friends along the way and have an enjoyable conversation over a meal. Those friendships may only last for the time it takes to have a cup of coffee and that is fine.

One caution...Smoking. While smoking indoors is not allowed, it is common in outdoor eating spaces. In North America, it would be normal for a non-smoker to want to distance themselves from the smoke. In Spain, and much of Europe, you will encounter individuals, even many very healthy and athletic individuals, who smoke and don't think twice about lighting up around others. If you can, accept it with a smile and have a nice conversation then move on and away later. This is Spain. You are here to experience Spain even if that means being around some less-than-perfect air for a few minutes.

Building Friendships:

When walking the Camino, it is fun to have brief snippets of conversation with others. These little bits of conversation can evolve into a more sustained Camino friendship.

In all probability, you will see others you have met on the trail repeatedly, although there can sometimes be days in between. A friendly reminder that you know them from a prior conversation and remember where they are from will gain many social points. Simply say something like; *"Buen Camino, Australia"* (if that is where they were from), *"Good morning, Ohio"*, and so on. This will let them know that you remember them and have taken the care to remember something about them such as where they are from.

If walking by yourself, you will likely be alone for the first day or two. If you choose to partake in small bits of conversation along the trail, by the end of your second or third day, you can build enjoyable friendships with other pilgrims. This can happen by simply walking along with another person or group for a kilometer or so, or by sharing coffee at one of the many stops.

Photos:

If you are walking by yourself, you will likely want to be included in some photos of the countryside and historical sights. Most other fellow pilgrims will be very happy to use your camera or cell phone to take your photo. Just remember to offer the same service and courtesy in return. Asking for someone to take your photo is not rude, and it is commonly done on the Camino.

The Camino can be as social or as solitary as you choose. Even when walking alone and desire time for personal mental reflection, it is comforting to know that other friendly pilgrims are always nearby.

There is a social downside to booking longer walks with a Camino agency.

If you have pre-booked lodging for every night along a multi-week hike, you are likely to find that friends you meet along the way are scheduled to stay in a different town. This creates the unfortunate situation of having to separate from your new acquaintances and likely not seeing them again.

Recommendation:

Consider NOT have a Camino travel service book everything for you on weeks longer than 1 week unless you are walking the French Way in high season.

~ ~ ~ ~ ~ ~

Simple Pleasures While on The Camino:

In addition to the enjoyable social aspects of the Camino, you will encounter many other, unexpected delights.

When walking the Camino, some of the great joys are in the small things. Watch and listen for them. This walk is more than simply finding your way to Santiago de Compostela. It is about paying attention to the sights and sounds around you. Many of your greater Camino memories will come from such elements as those listed here:

- **Cuckoo Birds**

    These delightfully sounding birds are common through much of the Camino de Santiago. As you head into Galicia, the region of Spain which includes Santiago, you will hear them as they flit from tree to tree. You might want to find a place to sit along the trail and listen to them.

- **Cow Bells and Cows on the Camino**

    In many sections of the Camino, you will walk near small farms and forest areas that have small herds of cows. Often the sound of cowbells will ring out as the cows go about their grazing.

    At times, you may find that you are sharing the Camino with a herd of cows, their shepherd, and a watchful dog. Stand back a bit and watch the small parade.

- **Wine, Bread and Olives**

    During dinners, you will find that table wine, both red and white, are often served with your meal at little or no additional cost. Give it a try. The wines of the region vary greatly, and many are quite good.

    Along with your wine, enjoy the wonderful variety of bread. Plates of bread of differing types are often placed before you, again at no additional cost. Enjoy it.

    Olive plates. Another great specialty. Bowls full of green olives often accompany and enhance your meal.

- **Small Churches**

    Many villages will have a small church. Some barely hold thirty or more people. Take a moment to step inside and appreciate these old buildings as they are often a focal point of the village. Each village church will have its own charm and history. In many cases, you will find that you can obtain a stamp for your Camino passport within the church. Maybe you will even be able to ring the church bell.

- **The Villages**

    Perhaps the greatest simple pleasure is the variety and availability of the many villages. Some of the villages house only a few people, other villages may be home to several hundred individuals. Stop in the local café or bar (bars are not just for liquor), get a coffee and snack, and just enjoy the local ambiance.

    It is helpful to understand that many of Spain's villages are poor and villagers have left for the cities, leaving many abandoned buildings behind. Some villages are nearly ghost towns which is a shame. When possible, try to help these enclaves out by stopping to buy a meal, pay for a Camino sellos (stamp) at a small church or even stay at a local albergue.

- **Camino Monuments and Art**

    Most segments of the Camino will have one or more monuments and statues to the Camino or to Saint James. Some are deeply religious in nature; many others are there simply to celebrate and honor the Camino. Stop and admire them and, while you are at it, share photo opportunities with other pilgrims.

Set your Fitbit aside and…
Relax – Look – Stop Often – Listen – Make Friends

15: **Your Shell, Pilgrim Passport and Compostela**

 A Camino shell, Credencial and Compostela are 3 unique attributes to this adventure.

Your Camino Shell:

Years ago, every pilgrim who reached Santiago de Compostela received a scallop shell from the church as a memento to their pilgrimage. They could then wear the shell on their hat or pack and take it home with them. <u>The shell represented that the person's life had changed,</u> and they were returning as a different person.

Traditions have changed, and many Camino pilgrims now carry one or more shells TO Santiago de Compostela instead of away from it. Carrying a shell can mean whatever you want to put into it.

If you wish to carry the shell simply as a mark that you are walking the Camino and as a souvenir of your adventure, that is fine. It can also signify a much deeper religious or emotional meaning which is defined separately by every Pilgrim.

Some individuals carry more than one shell to honor a loved one, maybe a deceased loved one. You may carry a small shell in anticipation of the birth of a child. Shells, by the way, do come in different sizes and almost all come with a cord to easily affix it to your pack.

You may choose to not carry a shell at all, and that is fine as well.

> *There is absolutely no need to order a shell before embarking on your Camino adventure!*

Where to get Camino Shells: You will find them in a multitude of places. The Camino shells are sold by street vendors, in bars, or in shops along the Camino. While most shells are plain or carry a mark of the cross or the Camino, some are highly decorated. There is no specific protocol with which you need concern yourself nor will anyone take issue with decorations on your Camino shell.

Cost: Camino shells typically cost around 2 to 3 Euros, although this can differ, especially for shells which sport significant decorations.

> ## *Camino Shell Recommendation*
> *Obtain one AFTER you have walked for several days*
> *as a small reward for completing your first days of this*
> *adventure.*

~ ~ ~ ~ ~ ~

Your Camino Passport/Credencial:

In addition to your normal country passport, you will likely want to acquire a "Pilgrim Passport" or "Credencial." Completion of the Pilgrim Passport is required if you wish to receive your Compostela/Certificate at the end of your walk.

A Credencial is a heavy stock folded paper document which enables you to document your walk with ink stamps along your adventure. It provides proof to the Pilgrims Office in Santiago de Compostela that you have walked the required distance and shows you are eligible to receive your Compostela certificate.

Like everything else with the Camino, this enjoyable aspect of your trip is easy and stress-free, and it is not necessary to acquire one before departing for Spain.

- If you have signed up with a Camino travel service, a Pilgrim Passport will likely be mailed to you before you depart.

- If you are doing all of your own planning (DIY) and making all of your reservations, you may either:

  o Order one online through an online source such as the Camino Forum Shop. View the products section on the SantiagoDeCompostela.me website. The cost for a Camino Passport is about 2 Euros plus shipping. ALSO, this site provides plastic covers for your pilgrim passport. This is important if you wish to keep this document in good shape.

OR

  o Wait until you arrive at your starting town on the Camino then ask the individual at the front desk of your hotel or Albergue. Many Albergues sell them and, if they don't, they will be able to direct you to a local shop or bar who does. The only downside to this plan is that it leaves you with one more task to complete after you arrive and before you start your walk.

Where to Get Your Passport Stamped

The quick answer regarding where to obtain "sellos", stamps for your Camino Passport, is almost anywhere. Most bars/restaurants, inns, churches, historical sites, and even some roadside stops will provide them.

Don't be shy. Ask if they will stamp your Camino passport. Every business and church along the Camino is used to this.

Often, you will need to put your own stamp into your Camino passport. Again., don't be shy. Just look around and you will probably see a rubber stamp and inkpad sitting on a table, a bar or on the counter. Caution, often there is little or no ink available in the ink pad and it may be dry.

Stamp Requirements

To receive your Compostela (certificate of distance) document at the end of your walk in Santiago de Compostela, *a few basic requirements must be met per the guidelines of the church and pilgrim's office.*

- <u>East of Sarria for the French Way or South of Tui for the Portuguese Way</u> - Obtain a minimum of 1 stamp per day. You may obtain more if you desire. Be aware that you could use up available space in your Camino Passport if you are not careful.

   Ideally, though not required, you would have one stamp per day from a church. Also, note that it is acceptable to have more than one Camino Passport if you find you have filled the original one before reaching Santiago.

- <u>Sarria to Santiago de Compostela (or Tui to SDC)</u> - Obtain a minimum of 2 stamps per day, ideally one from a church.

- DATED: All stamps should bear a date. In most cases, you will be expected to write in the date yourself and not the merchant.

Paying for Stamps

There is normally no charge to obtain a stamp for your pilgrim passport. In a few cases, where providing a stamp is the sole revenue source for a local entrepreneur, a donation of 1 Euro may be asked for. This is rare, however.

Tipping is a courtesy you may wish to extend to merchants from whom you have not purchased anything, but still desire a stamp.

Pace Yourself

Don't overdo the collection of stamps/sellos in your Compostela.

You do not want to run out of available spaces. Look at the available number of spaces in the document and the number of days you will be walking and then plan accordingly. If is far too common for fresh Pilgrims to want to obtain numerous stamps early in their trek, only to run out of room in the final days of walking. OR, go ahead and have fun with collecting as many as you wish, knowing that you may need more than one Camino Passport before your trek is complete.

A Few Helpful Supplies

Seriously consider packing along the following three items:

- Neck Wallet. A security neck wallet has multiple purposes. One helpful use with neck wallets is they are a wonderful way to keep your pilgrim passport handy and in good condition. You may also want to carry your own country passport and some cash in the neck wallet.

- Stamp pad. As mentioned above, the stamp pads in the various bars and churches are often dry of ink. Consider packing in your neck wallet a small stamp pad of your own. Doing so will ensure a supply of available ink. Do use the provided stamp pad when available as they come in a variety of colors, resulting in a visually appealing array final document.

- Pen. As you often need to enter the dates next to the stamps yourself, consider having a pen available. You may want to carry more than one as you will likely be asked by other pilgrims if they may borrow yours. You might not always get it back.

~ ~ ~ ~ ~ ~

Your Camino Compostela and Certificate of Distance:

At the completion of your hike into Santiago de Compostela, you will likely want to receive official documentation of your trip. Two documents are now provided:

- Compostela: The original document which shows you have completed this walk and met the minimal requirements.

- <u>Certificate of Distance</u>: This document provides more detail as it includes your arrival date, the trail you hiked, your starting date, and your starting point.

    To receive these documents, you must present your Camino Passport (Credencial). This proves by the stamps and dates on it that you have completed the minimum requirements.

<u>You May Need to Get A Number</u>

Starting during the Summer of 2019, the Pilgrim's Office began a new process of handing out numbers at the entrance instead of having you just get in a long line.

This does mean the following good and bad things:

- When the numbers for the day are handed out (this can happen early in the day), your opportunity to get a ticket is done and you will have to wait until the following day.
- This may increase the need to have one full day in SDC at the end of the walk.
- If you can, get in line to obtain your number very early in the morning.
- On the positive side, this eliminates the need to stand in a long line for hours. Now, you can just get your number and then go check into your hotel, get a meal and relax for a bit before going back to the Pilgrim's office.
- Note, as of this writing, this is a fairly new process and it is expected to evolve. It is likely that this may be instituted only during the busy months, but this scheduling is currently uncertain.

Obtaining your Compostela

When you arrive in Santiago de Compostela, you will want to work your way to the "Pilgrim's Welcome Office / Oficina del Peregrino" which is a short walk from the cathedral. Once there, you will be guided to where to get in line to receive your documents or obtain a ticket with a number on it. (new process – see box on the previous page)

One great way of avoiding this line is to wait until the morning after you arrive to obtain your number and, hopefully, get into the office early so you have the rest of the day to explore.

If you wish to receive your documentation on the day of your arrival, as most pilgrims do, don't dawdle when you come into town. Head to the office as soon as you can. Once this is done, you can then the take time to check into your hotel and explore this historic city at your leisure.

After receiving your documents, consider acquiring a short cardboard tube to put them in. These are available at the office and many gift shops. They do a great job of protecting these important items.

~ ~ ~ ~ ~ ~

16: **Your Final Camino Day**

The final day of your Camino. You are almost there. You have walked for days or weeks and you are now on the home stretch into Santiago de Compostela.

This last day brings a bit of excitement, sadness, and even some letdowns as you finish your trek. This day and the final stretch of your Camino is an unusual one and differs substantially from your preceding days in many regards.

The Camino Frances and the Camino Portuguese enter the city of Santiago de Compostela from different directions, but both trails end in the cathedral plaza. The last five to ten kilometers for both trails are through city and suburb streets. This is generally fine, just far different from previous days.

If you are hiking the Camino Frances, your last day will typically be under twenty kilometers, depending on where you spend your final night on the Camino. Your day is likely to start with a walk up to the Santiago de Compostela airport and then you will walk around it. This walk around the airport is surprisingly pleasant, given where it is.

The description of a walk around an airport, through suburbs and busy city streets may sound unappealing. This really isn't the case. While the walk is truly different, you will find that the Camino planners have done a good job of keeping the trail along fairly attractive and varied scenery.

Other Camino ways, such as the Northern Way, merge with the French Way on this last day. You are likely to have the opportunity to chat with others about their experiences on the other trails. You can gain some first-hand insights into these other paths, should you be considering another walk in the future.

The last kilometer takes you into the heart of historic Santiago de Compostela where you find yourself surrounded by tourists and tour groups. Now you may even be the focus of curiosity from those who have only heard about the Camino. Be prepared to be the subject of photos taken by curious and likely envious tourists as they watch people who are in the process of completing a long and wonderful trek.

When you enter the city of Santiago de Compostela on the French Way, you will find a large red-lettered sign with the city name. This is a great spot to have a photo taken with you and the sign as it somewhat commemorates the last stage of your hike.

~ ~ ~ ~ ~ ~

Reward Yourself with a Great Hotel Stay:

If your budget allows consider rewarding yourself with a great hotel stay in Santiago de Compostela.

Several historic hotels are in the center of the old town and close to the cathedral and many restaurants.

For full details on all hotels in Santiago de Compostela, check TripAdvisor.com, Booking.com or one of the many detailed travel guides. On sites such as Trip Advisor, you will find reviews, photos, and in-depth information on each hotel.

- Parador de Santiago de Compostela. The absolute top-end for hotels here and right on the main square.

- Hospederia San Martin Pinario. While not a 5-star hotel, this converted monastery provides a memorable stay and is very close to the cathedral.

- San Francisco Hotel Monumento. A block from the cathedral in a converted convent.

~ ~ ~ ~ ~ ~

The Botafumeiro and Pilgrim Mass:

The cathedral in Santiago is undergoing restoration as of this book's October 2019 update. In the past, this was a wonderful event to celebrate at the end of your hike. It was typically held on Friday evenings. It now will NOT reconvene until mid or late 2020.

The cathedral may still be visited however many areas are closed for repairs.

A daily pilgrim's mass is held at noon. Since work on the cathedral began, the mass has been moved to the Church of San Francisco a short walk from the cathedral.

~ ~ ~ ~ ~

You have arrived. Your Camino has been completed. You have obtained your Credencial and given yourself a celebratory toast.

Congratulations!

17 : Laundry

Doing laundry regularly is probably not your first choice of things to do. You will soon learn that it is a good practice to wash a few items every day right after checking into your hotel or albergue. This has the key advantages of:

- You will need to pack far fewer items.
- By washing right away in the afternoon, the items will generally be dry and ready by the time you leave the next morning.

Not every inn will have laundry service, machines or laundry soap. Be prepared to do regular washing in the washbasin in your hotel room. This should only take a few minutes, but a bit of preparation is advised. You should also have a supply of Euro coins of various values readily available as they will be needed if you choose to use washers or dryers. You cannot always count on the front desk having the ability to provide the necessary change.

Washing machine cost: An oddity along the Camino is the high cost of using washing machines and dryers in your lodging. While most costs along the Camino are reasonable to quite low, for some reason, the cost of using laundry machines is quite high.

For this reason alone, it is recommended that you hand wash a few items in your room instead of using machines on most days.

Recommended Supplies:

Have the following available in your luggage or backpack:

- A liquid detergent such as a Sports laundry detergent is advised. Roux Maison is one brand that works well for this purpose. The key thing is to pack a small quantity of a sports laundry detergent in your suitcase or backpack to enable you to use for hand laundering.

- Hangers and clips. Many inns do not provide clothes hangers. By bringing a few clothes hangers[8], and clips which can be attached to them, you will be ready to hang out your items in the shower or over the tub after they have been washed.

  These clips will also come in handy to hang a few items from your daypack as you continue on your hike. It is common to see others walking along the trail, with several items of clothing hanging out to dry as they work their

---

[8] Consider acquiring a small supply of inflatable or foldable clothes hangers. These provide great functionality while taking minimal space in your pack.

way along the Camino.

The Clothes You Select Matter

Bottom-line, leave all cotton clothes at home.

Don't pack or wear jeans, cotton shirts or even cotton under garments. Only take polyester or clothing of other synthetic material. They are lighter, moisture wicking, and dry much quicker than cotton. Sources such as REI, L.L. Bean, Eddie Bauer or Columbia provide a variety of these items.

~ ~ ~ ~ ~ ~

18: **When Nature Calls...**

This topic alone may prove the content in this book is geared toward the mature walker. To put it simply, as we age, the need for a bathroom stop increases. For a younger walker, this is often not something worth planning around. For a mature walker, the need of available facilities increases and the lack of them can quickly ruin a day.

The good news is you are generally within three to five kilometers from a bar or restaurant where you can use the facilities. You will find increased frequency of toilets as you get closer to Santiago de Compostela. If you are walking across the Meseta[9], the distances between available toilet

---

[9] The Meseta, Spain's high plains, is a section of the French Way which is not addressed in this book simply because it is much further east than the starting point of Astorga recommended for a 2 week walk.

stops can be fairly lengthy and caution should be taken.

One thing to note, is often the greatest distance without availability facilities is in the morning as you leave the village and work your way along the Camino. Put another way... go light on that first coffee and meal in the morning.

Always Carry Toilet Paper with You

It is quite common to enter a stall only to find that no paper is available, and no one is near to help you out.

There is some truth to saying of:
"There are more toilets than rolls of toilet paper on the Camino!"

Keep two rolls in your daypack or backpack and have them easily accessible. They should be kept in a waterproof container such as a gallon size Ziploc. Plan on bringing a roll to most restrooms along the trail and expect to find others around you asking to "borrow" it.

You may find that the "borrowed" rolls soon become community property, thus the suggestion that you keep an extra one handy. Don't feel self-conscious as you stand in line with a roll of toilet paper in your hand. Many others will be doing the same or envying you for being prepared.

Using "the Bush"

Heading into the bush or stepping behind a tree to "do

your business" may sound like an easy and common thing to do, but there are far fewer opportunities than you may expect. Don't count on being able to find a hidden spot. It might not materialize.

Don't let this deter you and keep you from walking the Camino. Just plan accordingly and know that there is generally an available rest stop a kilometer or two away. Worst case, you may have to do your thing in a spot which is a bit more open than you desire. This is something you will spot others doing from time to time as you walk the Camino.

Tipping for Toilet Usage

Pay toilets are not common. You will find many places ask you to leave a donation of 50 cents or 1 Euro for the privilege of using their facilities if you are not purchasing a meal or drink during your stop. Have a few Euro coins handy just for this purpose.

Eat Minimally to Avoid Problems

A simple measure to keep problems from occurring is simply to eat little at each stop and also drink moderately. This is, as cited earlier, especially true with your first morning meal. Just pace your eating and liquid intake and plan on making two or more quick meal/rest/potty stops during each day.

~ ~ ~ ~ ~ ~

19: **Safety Measures**

The Camino is relatively safe, but issues can and do arise. Safety concerns when traveling are natural and often appropriate, so a few precautions are in order.

You are likely the safest along the trail and in the villages. When traveling through the larger towns such as Porto or even through Santiago de Compostela, some issues with panhandlers and petty thieves can come up.

Pickpockets, for example, are adept and active in the larger towns so, when in crowds or visiting an ATM, be alert.

Recommendations to make your trip safer:

1. Leave your credit and debit cards at home. Yes, most credit cards offer theft protection, but it might be days before you realize a card has been lost or stolen.

   Recommendation: Consider acquiring a limited-use debit card from a local bank, a card which is pin-code protected. Pre-load the card with a set amount then, if needed, most cards will allow you to add funds via online transfer. By using these cards, your maximum loss will be the amount of funds you have pre-loaded into it. Caution, as cited earlier, make sure that the card is valid in Europe.

2. Neck wallet: Acquire a neck or belt wallet to hold your passport and some (not all) of your cash. This is also a great place to keep your Camino passport and your international passport.

3. Distribute your cash: Don't keep all of your cash in one place. Consider splitting it across your neck wallet, your day pack, and some in a zippered-pocket. This way, if a problem occurs with one part of your money stash, you will always have other money readily available.

4. Remove financial apps: If you are taking a smartphone with you on which you keep apps on it for such things as banking, Pay Pal, or your stock portfolio, remove and uninstall all of the apps which you will not need on the Camino before departing on your trip. If your phone does get lost or stolen, this will greatly remove your worry about unwanted intrusions into your primary financial sources.

5. Stay in sight of other pilgrims: You are generally near other pilgrims. By being in sight of one or more fellow pilgrims, the potential of issues arising decreases significantly.

6. Keep in touch with home: Have a designated individual back home who you have arranged to contact regularly. By doing this, you will have someone watching out for you should you run into problems. Do make sure that this

contact person knows you might not be able to contact them every day as some inns and albergues do not have adequate Wi-Fi.

7. <u>Medicines:</u> As with your cash, it is wise to split any medicines you are taking with you into different places. By putting a portion into your daypack and keeping a portion on you, you will never run the risk of being without important medicines.

8. <u>Medical kit</u>: Have a small medical kit with you. Blisters, indigestion, and other problems are common along the Camino.

> *Yes, you can drink the water but do carry some with you... just in case.*

Concerns about safety for a Camino trip should not keep you from going. As cited before, this is a relatively safe place and endeavor for men and women. Just take a few basic precautions as you would for any vacation and travels into new countries and places.

~ ~ ~ ~ ~ ~

20 : **After Your Walk**

Build in some tourist time. Northern Spain and the region of Galicia are historical and scenic treasure troves.

You have taken the time to travel a great distance and likely paid for expensive airfares. So, if your schedule allows, build in a bit more into your adventure on top of your Camino.

What and where you tour will depend on your personal preferences and budget. The good news is you can pack in a wide variety of experiences for minimal time and money. Another bit of good news is the great transportation system can get you out and about easily.

First and foremost, build in at least a full day to tour and explore the historical old city area of Santiago de Compostela, a UNESCO World Heritage site. After becoming acquainted with Santiago, you may want to consider the following daytrips if you have built in some extra time.

~ ~ ~ ~ ~ ~

Finisterre – the "End of the World"

Having just completed your Camino in Santiago de Compostela, it is reasonable to want to visit the ultimate end of the trail, Finisterre (or Fisterra) and its lighthouse. This visit can be accomplished by another week of walking. For most of us a daytrip will accomplish our goal.

A daytrip to Finisterre is actually something of a triangle as it also should also include a visit to the town of Muxia. Muxia is about a 30-minute drive from Finisterre. All combined, the trip to Finisterre, a visit to the lighthouse, and the jaunt to Muxia will take five to six hours including a stop for a relaxing seaside lunch.

There is no train to Finisterre and taking the bus is not advised due to the limited number of options and the time required to travel all the way to the lighthouse and "Mile 0." The best way to take this trip is either to rent a car in Santiago de Compostela or to take one of the many day tours offered.

Check www.TripAdvisor.com for a list of companies offering day tours. Example firms providing this service include:

- Viator.com
- UltreyaTours.com (visit their "Day Tours" page)
- DiscoverGalicia.es

~ ~ ~ ~ ~ ~

A Coruna

A short train ride to the north of Santiago de Compostela is the coastal city of A Coruna (also referred to as La Coruna). While this city has much to offer, a top attraction is the reconstructed ancient Roman lighthouse and the surrounding parks. Note, this lighthouse is not the same one you would visit by traveling to Finisterre.

To travel to the lighthouse, simply catch a taxi at the train station in A Coruna. For less than ten Euros, you can take the taxi out to this site. Plan on spending about three hours here, or more if you wish to explore the many trails in the large park. The tourist office at the entrance to this monument will gladly call a taxi for you when you are ready to depart for the train station or other sections of town.

Among the many other historical sites in this city, is the childhood home of Picasso and the wharves. Do build in visits to these locations if your schedule allows.

Trains between A Coruna and Santiago de Compostela run frequently, and it is generally not necessary to make advanced reservations. To get to the Santiago de Compostela train station, a taxi from your hotel is recommended.

By adding in an extra day or two, your trip will be enriched greatly with the addition of many wonderful memories.

~ ~ ~ ~ ~ ~

21 : **Packing Tips**

You need less than you may think. The first rule of packing for your Camino is a simple one...put back half of what you want to take. Pack light, even if you are using a suitcase and having it shipped from town-to-town.

> *It is easy to stress over and pack for every possible situation.*
> *Don't do it!*

Remember that you will be doing laundry along the way. Also keep in mind that, even in the churches and hotels along the way, everyone is used to working with Camino pilgrims who are dressed for the trail. There is little need to pack both trail and normal street clothes.

This book does not outline item-by-item all of what you should take, especially as it pertains to clothing. There are, however, some basic guidelines and suggestions you may wish to follow. Several suggestions have been made in this book and they are summarized here along with tips on a few essentials to consider.

It is also important to keep in mind that <u>you can find every conceivable service and store along the Camino</u>. If you find you have forgotten something of note, chances are you will find it in many of the towns on your route. These stores are generally immediately on the Camino route, so you will not have to look far for: sporting goods, pharmacies, clothing, snacks or other items.

A few suggestions and packing tips:

1. <u>Trekking Poles:</u> Having a set of light-weight trekking poles with you can be invaluable. If you have not used them in the past, don't worry. You won't be the first person who does a few awkward maneuvers in trying to figure them out. Inexpensive trekking poles, or simple walking sticks, are available in many stores along the way, should you forget to purchase them in advance.

2. <u>Daypack or Backpack:</u> Your pack should include the following:

   o Ability to attach trekking poles from the FRONT. Most daypacks will enable you to attach poles from the back which sounds fine but does not work well in practice. You want to be able to access your poles while walking and you want to be able to store them away while walking. Often, a simple solution is to attach a pair of carabiners to a loop at the front straps and then allow you to tuck the bottom ends of your poles to the sides of your pack. Some testing and adjustments will likely be needed.

o   Ability to hang wet clothes. Make sure your pack has clips which enable you to hang wet clothes out while you walk.

o   Water access. Make sure you have either a water bladder with a tube to drink from or easy access to a water bottle. You don't want to have to stop and take your pack off every time you need a drink.

o   Open weave outer pocket. Your laundry might not always be dry by morning. Having a large outer pocket with an open weave will allow you to air out damp items.

3.   Neck Wallet: This was mentioned earlier in the book and is worth repeating. Acquire a neck wallet which is about 5" wide and 7" tall. Having a neck wallet with you at all times will give you easy access to your Camino Passport, your real passport, and a portion of your cash supply. Remember to tuck the neck wallet under your shirt when out in public.

4.   Twist Ties: Having a few twist ties, or similar items, along with you can be very helpful to solve a number of needs, such as hanging clothing or trekking poles from your daypack.

5.   Stamp Pad and Pen: Having your own stamp pad and pen will ensure that you will be able to get a good stamp into your passport at each stop. These would likely be carried

in your neck wallet during your trek.

6. <u>Rain Jacket or Poncho:</u> You don't need both a jacket and a poncho You will probably need one of them, especially if you are hiking in the Spring. The ideal rain jacket will have a hood and also have the ability to zip open the sides below the arms for better ventilation.

7. <u>Rain Pants</u>: If traveling in the winter or early spring, a pair of rain pants is advised as Galicia in Spain and the Portuguese Way are near the ocean and unexpected rainfalls often occur.

8. <u>Shoes – 3 Types</u>: You will, of course, want to have a sturdy pair of shoes, probably hiking shoes or similar. In addition, bring along a comfortable pair of shoes to wear in town and in restaurants in the evening after your walk. You may also want to have a pair of flip-flops as these can come in handy with some shower situations.

o <u>Shoes for the French Way</u> It is hilly enough, for most of us, sturdy hiking shoes are warranted. DO make sure you have worn in your hiking shoes before beginning your Camino. Starting the trek with a new pair of hiking or walking shoes is a sure way to incur large and painful blisters.

o <u>Shoes for the Portuguese Way</u> The stretch from Tui to SDC is fairly gentle and many individuals find that lighter weight shoes, even sandals, are acceptable. Consider wearing one type of shoe while keeping the other in your pack to allow for the differing types of walk you will encounter.

9. Socks: The author recommends Merino Wool or similar light weight and durable socks. There are several good brands. These socks are sturdy and will not overheat most people's feet. Three pair are recommended. One can be kept in your suitcase. A spare pair should always be in your pack in case the pair you are wearing gets wet during your walk. REMEMBER wet or damp feet cause blisters so you will only want socks made of wicking material.

10. Medical Kit: Small medical problems are common, especially blisters. Bring with you a small kit. It should include a variety of bandages and wraps for the variety of blisters which can occur. Purchase blister pads which medicate in addition to protecting the blister.

    It is also helpful to have medicines for digestive issues.

11. Sun Protection: You are likely to encounter strong sun as you work your way along the Camino. A supply of sunscreen and lip protection is advised.

12. Swiss Army Knife: You don't need a real fancy one. Having a small knife which includes a screwdriver and a few other tools can be of great help as issues arise. Do note that this should not be carried onboard any flight. Any knife or similar item should only be put into checked luggage.

13. Non-Cotton Clothing: Mentioned before. Leave all cotton fabric clothes at home, including jeans, bras and underwear. You only want to take lightweight items that

wick and can be easily washed and dried along the trail.

14. <u>Zip-off Pants</u>: Consider bringing along one pair of long pants that have zippers near the knees and enable you to convert the long pants to shorts. This provides the flexibility you will need during the day and reduces the total number of items you need to bring.

15. <u>Laundry Detergent</u>: Bring along a small supply of a sports wash which can be used to hand wash clothes at the end of each day's walk. The author recommends Roux Maison as an excellent product for hand washing clothes.

16. <u>Hangers and Clips</u>: Bring a few hangers and clips to use each evening to hang up the items you have washed. You might even want to bring a short cord so you can set up an impromptu clothesline.

    To conserve space in your pack or suitcase, purchase folding or inflatable hangers. Many of these

17. <u>Hat:</u> You will likely encounter substantial sun along your trek. To protect yourself, pack a lightweight, broad-brim hat to provide protection from the sun and can easily be scrunched into your pack.

18. <u>Guidebook:</u> Not essential but helpful. Consider bringing along one of the more popular guidebooks (see reference section). Having one along can be helpful each evening as you plan your next day's walk.

19. <u>Power Converter:</u> Spain is on the 220 volt system vs. the United States which is 110 volt for most uses. If you plan on taking along a laptop, hair dryer or similar appliance,

you will want to buy a simple power converter. NOTE, this is not needed for most cellphones as they work equally well with 110 or 220. You will want to have a 220 volt plug adapter for any and all devices which you use in Spain.

20. Toilet Paper: Bring 2 rolls with you in your pack and replace as needed throughout your hike.

21. Daypack Cover: Brief rains are common in the Galicia region. If you are not packing a poncho which would double as a cover for your daypack, consider packing a cover for your daypack these are light weight, easy to use and take far less room in your pack than a poncho.

The above is not a comprehensive list of items to pack although it should provide some helpful tips on what to bring. It also bears repeating that there are many small stores along your route where you may acquire items you may have forgotten before departing for Spain.

~ ~ ~ ~ ~ ~

Resources

A list of references, resources and helpful guides follow. To help you finalize your planning, this section lists all of the travel and Camino references cited throughout this book. This is not an exhaustive list nor is this intended to be a list of the best resources. This is simply a list of proven sites and references.

Similar to the packing tip suggestion of pack light, you may want to do the same when it comes to how many books, apps, and reference sites you work with. Keeping it mentally light is just as important as packing light.

Ideally, this book will have given you most of the guidance you need to plan your Camino. If not, the list of resources cited here should fill any information gaps you may have.

Books: Consider acquiring just **one** of the following:

- *"A Pilgrim's Guide to the Camino de Santiago"* by John Brierley.

- *"Camino de Santiago – Practical Preparation and Background"* by Gerald Kelly

- *"Camino de Santiago Village to Village Guide"* by Anna Dintaman and David Landis

Apps: (Only one is needed)

- *"Camino Pilgrim"* A highly recommended app that provides details for each day's walk and interactive mapping. This is available both for Apple iPhone and Android phones.

  OR

- *"Camino de Santiago Guide"* A well-rated free app which provides detailed trail and town guidance.

- There are also apps available for luggage transfer, albergues, and ground transportation.

Camino Travel Service:

- CaminoWays.com - This service provides a wide range of support and programs. Highly recommended if you are not wanting to set up everything yourself.

- MacsAdventure.com - Another well regarded Camino trip planning service/packager, providing a good range of support and travel options.

- FrescoTours.com - This firm provides both guided tours and self-guided Camino walks.

- MarlyCamino.com - Guided tours geared to a variety of

ability levels.

- <u>Backroads.com.</u> Guided tours which also combine touring of the surrounding area. A bit more expensive than many other services.

Transportation Websites:

- <u>Train Travel:</u>
  - o <u>Rome2Rio.com</u> – covers all/most modes of ground transportation.
  - o <u>RailEurope.com</u> - Use for train schedules and reservations.
  - o <u>Renfe</u>.com – the Spanish rail system.
  - o <u>Trainline</u>.eu – train schedules and reservations.
  - o <u>GoEuro</u>.com – includes train and bus schedules and reservations.

- <u>Bus Service:</u>
  - o <u>GoEuro.com</u> - bus service, including a service from Santiago airport to Sarria.
  - o <u>BusBud</u>.com - bus service to many Camino starting points.
  - o <u>Rome2Rio.com</u> - bus service, including a service from Santiago airport to Sarria.

- <u>Taxi and Shuttle:</u>
  - o <u>TaxiGalicia.com</u> - private transportation from Santiago airport to Sarria.
  - o <u>TourShuttle.com</u> - private transportation from

Santiago airport to Sarria.

o   AirportsTaxiTransfers.com - taxi or shuttle service from Santiago, Madrid, and other cities to many Camino starting points.

o   SunTransfers.com – taxi shuttle service from Santiago, Madrid and other cities to many Camino starting points.

o   BiarritzAirportTransfers.com – Use for ground transportation to St Jean Pied de Port in France, from the Biarritz airport.

Luggage Transfer Services: (Not needed if you are using a Camino travel service)

• JacoTrans.com

• ExpressBourricot.com - This firm also does passenger transport in several locations.

• TaxiBelorado.com

Camino Information Sites:

• WisePilgrim.com – a highly detailed list of albergues and inns for most towns and villages along the Camino.

• TripAdviser.com – Use this site to research inns and find reviews from other walkers.

• Booking.com (or similar such as Expedia or Travelocity) – Use to research inns and hotels and make reservations along the Camino.

• AmericanPilgrims.org – This site provides a detailed list

of information resources.

- SantiagoDeCompostela.me - Camino Forum Shop. Acquire a Pilgrim Passport here.

Finisterre Tours:

- Viator.com – This firm provides a variety of Finisterre and other group tours out of Santiago.

- CaminoWays.com – group tours to Finisterre geared to Camino pilgrims.

- UltreyaTours.com – similar to Viator. They offer a variety of tours out of Santiago including group tours to Finisterre.

~ ~ ~ ~ ~ ~

Works by BG Preston

Check out these other publications. B.G. Preston has published several recent works of fiction. Each of these works are:

- Available in print format through most leading providers.

- Written to provide some fun and adventure, along with a bit of education for the reader… a goal similar to *Camino Easy*, except that the following works are fiction.

BLUE WATER BEDLAM

4 clueless guys. A newish yacht. A boatload of trouble!

Charlie just wanted to have some fun with his new boat and share that fun with his friends. Little did the seasick prone, lotto winner, Charlie, know that he had bought into a whole lot of problems.

Four retired guys set forth on a boating adventure into

the beautiful Puget Sound. Knowing nothing about what it takes to handle a yacht and the news of a recent murder on board doesn't stop them. Soon, they find troubles well beyond anything they could expect or want.

Murphy's Law doesn't begin to cover what these guys are in for! Boating on the Puget Sound and the Inside Passage, they stumble into intrigue and adventure at every turn.

Look for *"Blue Water Bedlam"* in Amazon and other leading sites.

~ ~ ~ ~ ~ ~

CAMINO PASSAGES (Fiction)

NEW - February 2019.

The Camino de Santiago is an historical trail across northern Spain which provides hikers with an incredible variety of architectural, natural, and cultural delights. It also, as Larry Adams learns, a wonderful social journey as well.

Setting out for Spain, Larry is only seeking to have a solo adventure and a much needed change of pace. What Larry encounters during his walk are experiences and new relationships that could change his life forever.

Along the way, he meets a charming woman from France. Together, they visit many villages and historical locations as they enrich their understanding of this beautiful region and each other.

Camino Passages is a work of fiction but one which is rich in description and relationships.

This story will appeal to anyone who enjoys travel fiction and stories of personal development, regardless of the location. For individuals who are contemplating walking some or all of the Camino Frances, they will find many helpful suggestions built into the story.

Check out *Camino Passages* on Amazon and other leading sites.

~ ~ ~ ~ ~ ~

Buen Camino!

Please remember the Camino mantra of:

Have fun

Have an adventure

Don't kill yourself

Author's Facebook Page

Your feedback is always appreciated. Feel free to visit the author's Facebook page to post any questions or suggestions you may have.

www.Facebook.com/BGPreston.author

~ ~ ~ ~ ~ ~

Made in the USA
Monee, IL
19 November 2019

17100012R00085